SpringerBriefs in Economics

More information about this series at http://www.springer.com/series/8876

Jingyi Wang

The Past and Future of International Monetary System

With the Performances of the US Dollar, the Euro and the CNY

Springer

Jingyi Wang
Social Sciences Academic Press (China)
Chinese Academy of Social Sciences
Beijing
China

ISSN 2191-5504 ISSN 2191-5512 (electronic)
SpringerBriefs in Economics
ISBN 978-981-10-0163-5 ISBN 978-981-10-0164-2 (eBook)
DOI 10.1007/978-981-10-0164-2

Library of Congress Control Number: 2015956357

Printed on acid-free paper

This Springer imprint is published by SpringerNature
The registered company is Springer Science+Business Media Singapore Pte Ltd.

Thanks to My Husband and My Parents
for their Unconditional Support
and Continuing Encouragement,
and also to My Little Angell, for your lovely smile.

Acknowledgments

This book is based on my doctoral study which commenced at the Ph.D. Programme in Financial Systems, Risk Management and Regulation, in Università Degli Studi Guglielmo Marconi during the period of 2011–2014. In that period, I have been greatly supervised by Professor Paolo Savona and assisted by Professor Chiara Oldani in guiding my book on all aspects.

I am indebted to Professor Paolo Savona. He is a prestigious economist in Italy and worldwide, insightful and rich experienced both in academic research and in policy-making field. Among his research, the most significant one is attributed to the first econometric model of Italian economy, the first analyses on the international monetary base and Eurodollar, and on the macroeconomic effects of derivatives contracts, which have all anticipated in a systematic way the happening of the dramatic events experienced by the Italian and international economy in the last forty years. My research is a result of learning and absorbing the insightful ideas from him.

I really appreciate Università Degli Studi Guglielmo Marconi for financing me to completing my academic missions, such as visiting research in 2011. I sincerely thank to the support from the former deputy Director of the Institute of European Studies of Chinese Academy of Social Sciences, Professor Luo Hongbo, who strongly encouraged me to push my doctoral study forward.

Finally, I would like to thank my family for staying with me on the whole study.

Contents

1 Introduction 1

2 A Short Review on the International Monetary System 5
2.1 The History of International Monetary System. 5
2.2 Proposals on Reforming the IMS Studies 11
2.3 Research Question 15

3 Sovereign Dollar: "The Dollar Is Our Currency, but It's Your Problem" 19
3.1 Monetary System in the U.S 19
3.2 "The Dollar Is Our Currency, but It's Your Problem" 31

4 Regional Euro: "Creative, Ambitious, but Trapped" 35
4.1 Monetary System in the Eurozone 35
4.2 "Creative, Ambitious, but Trapped" 46

5 Rising CNY: "The Elephant in the Room" 51
5.1 Monetary System in China 51
5.2 Path Toward International Money 61

6 Supranational SDRs: Another Way Worth Trying? 65
6.1 The Methods for Establishing the SDRs and Its Working System 67
6.2 Another Way Worth Trying? 76

7 Conclusion 85
7.1 Summary 87
7.2 Added-Value of the Book 88
7.3 Limits of the Research Work and Future Research 88

Bibliography 89

Abstract

The aim of this book was to examine the problems of current International Monetary System, especially of the International Standard. The book firstly focuses on the different monetary systems of the current major moneys: the US dollar, the euro and the CNY; and concluded that as different experiences being a de facto international standard (or potentially), all the three could be grouped into (a) Sovereignty currency that equipped with "Triffin Dilemma" and "exorbitant privilege"; (b) Regional monetary integration that trapped by the unparallel development of economy and politics; and (c) Rising potential reserved currency who is inexperienced with the pace of internationalization. Secondly, the book examined the performance of the existent standard of international monetary system, the SDRs: equally introduce the characteristics of its monetary system and its trial for acting as a supranational international standard. Moreover in this section, the book tries to experiment the inclusion of CNY to the current SDRs system, to see the potential changes the system would have, thus proposing the SDRs' future reform.

The analytical research is mainly based on comparing the mechanisms and performances of major international standards in the current international monetary system. Their political/policy reactions and economic philosophies behind them are not only, to some extent, the reasonable response to the current international monetary system, but also the fundamental factors for deciding the forthcoming changes or reforms of a future international monetary system.

Keywords International Monetary System · The US dollar · The Euro · The CNY · The SDRs

Chapter 1
Introduction

The present international monetary system, is generally called the "post-Bretton Woods" system. Literally, it has inherited some features from its predecessor, the Bretton Woods system (1945–1971), which was established as a post-war arrangement and an attempt for reconstruction of the world financial order. In the "Bretton Woods" era, nations agreed to the regime of fixed but adjustable exchange rates where the currencies were pegged against the dollar, with the dollar itself convertible into gold at a fixed price. Two international institutions, the World Bank and the International Monetary Fund (IMF) were simultaneously created; their main functions were, respectively, to lend for investment projects in developing states and to rescue countries from the crucial moments in finance. Although the Bretton Wood system collapsed right after the unilateral default of the US government, the necessity of an international monetary system is still a consensus, especially under the current global highly instable situation. There is a reason lying in the objective of such an idea, that is to create an order that combined the benefits of a stable external system so as to provide the freedom for governments to pursue domestic policies aimed at promoting economic growth and social development.

In practice, the core components of an international monetary system should contain, among other things, the following three aspects: an international reserve standard played as an anchor in the system, some arrangements such as an agreed foreign exchange regime to help adjust each participant's international balance of payment, and accordingly global collaboration mechanism, like the practice from G7/8 to G20. All the three aspects are crucial for defining and evaluating an international monetary system. When it comes to understand the past and the current international monetary system so as to find out the right approach for the future one, it is quite sensible for this book to focus on those three components.

Actually, there are a number of blueprints about reestablishment of a new international monetary system in the future. Some of the views are on a traditional line, as in the speech of Governor of the People's Bank of China proposing to reinforce the use of Special Drawing Rights (SDRs)[1]; some are even radical, such

[1]On March 23, 2009, Mr. Zhou Xiaochuan-Governor of the People's Bank of China issued a far-reaching proposal for diversification away from the U.S. dollar in international standard toward a supranational currency based on the IMF's SDRs.

J. Wang, *The Past and Future of International Monetary System*,
SpringerBriefs in Economics, DOI 10.1007/978-981-10-0164-2_1

as more recently the 18-page of position proposed by Vatican.[2] Practically, an international monetary system is an arrangement backed by collaborated agreements rather than real global authority. However, the features of an international monetary system are always strongly influenced by the leading economic entities in its time. Actually, from time to time, whether in the era of pound or of the dollar in last century, or more recently of the multi-polar circumstance with the born of the euro, the marginal use of Japanese yen and the awaiting of the rise of Chinese yuan, there is by no means a powerful supranational monetary authority with any binding force, but rotated influential currency leaders. Therefore, to fully understand how an international monetary system operates or more profoundly, how it is accepted by all the members involved, thus looking forward a future one, it should be better look from the inside, especially begin the studies with realizing the leading currencies.

In order to start from an analytical ground and to be more comparable, institutional structures of different currencies and their economic conditions should be got into knowledge, thus understanding their rationality to collaborate in a system. There are three currencies which have been drawing the most attentions in the world nowadays: the most influential international liquidity and the de facto international reserve money, the US dollar; so far a new experiment, the euro, though facing challenges in a non-Optimal Currency Areas (OCAs); and the potential new that could change the status quo as a late entry backed by its rising power, the Chinese yuan. It is important to know their different mechanism in the field of monetary affairs, including the objective(s) and responsibilities of monetary authority, creation of base money and the monetary multipliers, thus making clear their institutional problems.

It is not surprised that in the era of post-Bretton Wood, especially most recently, neither the most sophisticated US dollar, nor the once powerful challenger the euro, and nor the seemly promising yuan shows proper policy reactions to solve either their domestic monetary problems or international ones. On one hand, the traditional international liquidities, represented by the dollar and the euro, are suffering confidence crisis; while on the other hand, the yuan is too premature to be an alternative one. As a consequence question on the issue of international monetary standard arise.

In the past, gold had been long and widely adopted as a world monetary standard especially in the era rested on the conversion of paper notes into pre-set quantities of gold. According to the classical definition, money has the responsibilities to be an intermediary of exchange (or international measurement of value), an instrument of savings, and a tool of domestic payments. Gold standard ensured the stability during most of commercial economy and the early stage of capitalism; however, it was confronted with embarrassment after unprecedented economic prosperity and waves of globalizations. The nature that helps it get the acknowledgement as a

[2]In this proposal released in late October, the Pontificate Council in Vatican calls for "New World Economic Authority" including a "Global Central Bank" and tax on the financial transaction.

perfect standard, in turn, prevents it from long being. The limit quantity of gold was no longer suitable for the world's further prosperity. Therefore, another "ever-lasting" international standard, the paper money, was introduced firstly in modern time by Britain then followed the US dollar after the crash of the pound sterling. This new kind of standard was created in order to avoid the shortage of gold and was guaranteed by, at that time, the strongest economic and political sovereignty behind it. Take the US dollar for example, despite times of "dollar shortage", this national currency standard served the world economy for decades however finally make a concession to its national interests of depreciation and freely floating. After that, the dollar-led international system goes on working till now under the "Washington Consensus" that labelled with a volatile exchange rate regime.

By the end of the first decade of new millennium, a seemly sudden onset of constant defaults in housing industry in the U.S. soon escalated into a banking turmoil. This contagion was quickly spread around the world through so-called financial innovations and finally drew most of the world into serious financial crisis and economic recession. The terrible crisis had pushed both the dollar and its backed system on the edge: the market confidence had been further weakened by the U.S.' rounds of Quantitative Easing policy (QEs) and the "dollar glut" that flooded to every corner of the world had threaten the credibility of this de facto international standard. More importantly, this crisis had exposed structural problems of the current system and its frangibility.

Consequently, there are more and more voices calling for reformation, starting from a re-establishment of a stable and accountable international standard. In this background, the SDRs, or "paper gold", which was firstly issued by the IMF in 1970, is highlighted among others. From learning the methods of its establishment, SDRs was designed to be a solution for the "Triffin Dilemma" at that time, that is to say, in order to supplement the shortage of gold as an international standard in a fixed exchange regime as well as to provide the sufficient international liquidity to support the world economic growth. However, short after that, forced by the domestic political and economic pressures, the U.S. unilaterally announced to give up the convertibility of the dollar to gold at a fixed price. This default was followed by general adoption of floating exchange regime and finally the collapse of the "Bretton Wood System". Given lack of rational arrangements and policy consensus among nations, the SDRs had taken marginal effects for a long time. Therefore, it is time to retrospect the establishment and the feasibility of the SDRs. What is the building methodology? What are its institutional governance and its working system? What would happen if the international standard changed into the SDRs? On the other hand, it is wise to understand in advance the intrinsic weaknesses that prevent the SDRs to perform as a sound international standard.

In the very beginning, these are the conflicts originated from the imbalance of trade and massive cross-border capital movements that beyond controlled. Apart from the leading country's soaring deficits and their consequences, there are opposite parties that suffer the pains also from external imbalance as well. Given the volatile exchange rate regime in the "post-Bretton Wood" era and the lessons from the Asian Financial Crisis in the late 1990s, most emerging countries adopted a pegged exchange rate regime where the value of the currency is tied to the U.S. dollar, or a basket of international moneys. This kind of policy gave them a more stable monetary parity when they tried to promote their economy by export-led development strategy. As a result, they accumulated a huge number of foreign exchange reserves. China, of course, is among the largest. However, this enormous amount of foreign reserves has become a "hot potato". The emerging country, take China for instance, is now under double pressures: the appreciation demand from outside and the inflation inside. Both of them can be traced the cause from the country's imbalance of payment. China took its comparative advantage of trade encouraging export and so had been gradually running an external surplus. However, the long-term pegged exchange rate policy prevented it from doing any adjustment in time before it becomes so hard-pressed. On the other hand, to keep a stable monetary parity against the dollar, China had to swallow the big amount of foreign exchange reserve at the expense of the passive expansion of its monetary base, running the risk of domestic inflation. For China, and other emerging countries alike, it is also a crucial time to adjust the external imbalance, rooting out the deep source of the problem.

Apart from all the facts that are widely accepted, there is an issue of the application of a sound international standard. However, it is the fundamental problem that rooted in the current system and triggered the economic crisis. Moreover, it calls for much more consideration, courage as well as wisdom of the international community.

Although it is proved that there is an urgent call for more stable international standard, and a deep demand for adjustment about the structural imbalance in the world economy, before we start our trying, there is a fundamental requirement for a new way of thinking, that is, to re-establish the collaboration following the geopolitical economics. Geopolitical economics is the discipline that applies to the world economy the principles of economics. In this view, any "beggar my neighbor" policy or isolations could not solve the problems we share in common. Instead, the feature of high degree of interactive activities among countries should be taken into considerations when a monetary authority is deciding and implementing its policy. Economic problems should be solved through very active and collaborated foreign policy. Every international market participant should hold its obligation to adjust the imbalance when it is necessary. As an organizer and supervisor, governments should be responsible for reinforcing the implement of the laws. Moreover, make good use of multilateral institutions such as IMF, G20 to practice a stable and workable international standard, to harmonize the worldwide foreign exchange rate regime, to establish necessary regulations on financial supervision in order to relief the contagion, and finally establish an orderly organized and stably worked international monetary system for mutual interests and all-win games.

Chapter 2
A Short Review on the International Monetary System

2.1 The History of International Monetary System

2.1.1 Definitions of International Monetary System

There is no clear definition on the international monetary system (IMS). As defined by Eichengreen (2008), the international monetary system is

> ...the glue that binds national economies together. Its role is to lend order and stability to foreign exchange markets, to encourage the elimination of balance-of-payments problems, and to provide access to international credits in the event of disruptive shocks.

Regarding to the relationship between the international monetary system and international financial system, Truman (2010) outlined

> the international monetary system is the set of rules, conventions, and institutions that govern and condition official actions and policies affecting the international economy and financial system: exchange rate regimes, intervention policies, the size and composition of reserve holdings, mechanisms of official financial support, etc. The international monetary system exists within the international financial system, which today is dominated by private, not publicactors and their balance sheets.

Dooley, Folkerts-Landau and Garber (2003) refer the international monetary system of today is

> ...composed of a core issuing the dominant international currency, and a periphery. The periphery is committed to export-led growth based on the maintenance of an undervalued exchange rate.

To sum up, the international monetary systems can be portrayed as: sets of rules and supporting institutions that facilitate international trade cross border investment and generally the reallocation of capital between nation states. It provides means of payment acceptable between buyers and sellers of different nationality, including deferred payment. To operate successfully, the system need to inspire confidence, to provide sufficient liquidity for fluctuating levels of trade and to provide means by

J. Wang, *The Past and Future of International Monetary System*,
SpringerBriefs in Economics, DOI 10.1007/978-981-10-0164-2_2

which global imbalances can be corrected. The systems can grow organically as the collective result of numerous individual agreements between international economic actors spread over several decades.

2.1.2 History of International Monetary System

Over the past 200 years, the international monetary system (IMS) has gone through many changes. From 1815 to 1873, IMS was operating by Bimetallism, which was followed by International Gold Standard till the outbreak of the First World War. From 1915 to 1999, IMS adopted Dollar–Gold Standard, Gold Exchange Standard, Dollar–Gold Standard, Dollar Standard, and Flexible Exchange Rates.

There were informal regimes existed before mid-1940s. The pound sterling was the premier international currency of the gold standard period. Historians estimate, for example that 60–90 % of the world's trade was invoiced in sterling in the 19th century (Broz 1997; Hale 1999). In 1899, the share of pound in known foreign exchange holdings of official institutions was more than twice the total of the next nearest competitors, the franc and the mark, and much greater than the dollar (Lindert 1969).

In the past, gold had been long and widely adopted as a world monetary standard especially in the era rested on the conversion of paper notes into preset quantities of gold. According to the classical definition, money has the responsibilities to be an intermediary of exchange (or international measurement of value), an instrument of savings, and a tool of domestic payments. Gold standard ensured the stability during most of commercial economy and the early stage of capitalism; however, it was confronted with embarrassment after unprecedented economic prosperity and waves of globalizations.

The nature that helps it get the acknowledgement as a perfect standard, in turn, prevents it from long being. The limit quantity of gold was no longer suitable for the world's further prosperity. Therefore, another "ever-lasting" international standard, the paper money, was introduced firstly in modern time by Britain then followed the US dollar after the crash of the pound sterling. This new kind of standard was created in order to avoid the shortage of gold and was guaranteed by, at that time, the strongest economic and political sovereignty behind it. Take the US dollar for example, despite times of "dollar shortage", this national currency standard served the world economy for decades however finally make a concession to its national interests of depreciation and freely floating. After that, the dollar-led international system goes on working till now that labelled with a volatile exchange rate regime.

The first single architectural vision of IMS is the Bretton Woods System in 1944. The Bretton Woods System was signed and became the first international institution to govern monetary relations among independent nation-states. It is a system established by negotiated rules for commercial and financial relations among the world's major economies. The chief features of the Bretton Woods system were an obligation for each country to adopt a monetary policy that maintained the exchange rate by tying its currency to the U.S. dollar and the ability of IMF to bridge temporary imbalances of payments. Under the Bretton Woods, nations agreed to the regime of fixed but adjustable exchange rates where the currencies were pegged against the dollar, with the dollar itself convertible into gold at a fixed price. The IMF and the World Bank (then called the International Bank for Reconstruction and Development) was established. These organizations became operational in 1945 after a sufficient number of countries had ratified the agreement.

In August 1971, the United States unilaterally terminated convertibility of the U.S. dollar to gold. This brought the Bretton Woods system to an end, and the dollar become fiat currency (Wlatz 1969; Calleo and Rowland 1973).This action created the situation in which the USD became a reserve currency used by many states. At the same time, many fixed currencies (such as GBP, for example), also became free floating. In the floating exchange rate regime, dollar as reserve currency has become the world's *fiatmoney*. As Savona and Viviani (2005) argued, the US should agree—at least in principle–on the necessity of a cooperative policy on exchange rates, to obtain a monetary standard governed by some rules. The absence of an international monetary standard created through an agreement transfers the burden of the adjustment from the US to the other countries or, worse yet, assigns the government of the exchange rates exclusively to the market.

By the introduction of the euro in 1990s, the convergence criteria for membership in the European Monetary Union, the merits and defects of the euro as an international rival to the dollar, and to the characteristics that have made past international currencies great as well. It goes on to consider the institutional gap in the world system arising from the absence of an official world currency and the threat to stability that arises in transition periods when the euro is phased in. It is expected that the introduction of the euro involve diversification from the dollar that will require multilateral attention to the dollar-euro exchange rate (Mundell 1998).

However, the financial crisis in eurozone since 2008 trigged one problem in the case of euro: that each eurozone country has a separate market for its government bonds, the most stable assets serving as benchmarks. Market depth and liquidity are thus lacking compared to the dollar (Eichengreen 2009).

Consequently, there are more voices calling for reformation, starting from a re-establishment of a stable and accountable international standard. In this background, the SDRs, or "paper gold", which was firstly issued by the IMF in 1970, is highlighted among others. According to the methods of its establishment, the SDRs was designed to be a solution for the "Triffin Dilemma" at that time, that is to say, in order to supplement the shortage of gold as an international standard in a fixed exchange regime as well as to provide the sufficient international liquidity to support the world economic growth. However, short after that, forced by the domestic political and economic pressures, the U.S unilaterally announced to give up the convertibility of the dollar to gold at a fixed price. This default was followed by general adoption of floating exchange regime and finally the collapse of the "Bretton Wood System". Given lack of rational arrangements and policy consensus among nations, the SDRs had taken marginal effects for a long time.

Apart from the application of a new international standard, a fundamental problem that rested in the current system and triggered the economic crisis calls for much more consideration, courage as well as wisdom of the international community. The diversification of the system is indispensable to keep accord with economic changes. It is the intrinsic requirement to enhance the stability of the system and to break away from monopoly monetary power. This is a great opportunity for CNY to internationalization.

The pace of internationalization of CNY has picked up in recent years with new currency swap agreements, clearing banks and CNY investment quotas being agreed in several financial centres.

Till 2012, the People's Bank of China (PBoC) has signed currency swap agreements with 18 central banks, valued at over 1.6 trillion (most recently with the Reserve Bank of Australia for an CNY200 billion three-year swap agreement). In 2011, about 10 % of China's total cross-border trade was settled in CNY compared to only 2 % in 2010. In 2013, the PBoC has set up currency swap agreements with the European Central Bank at CNY350 billion follows similar agreements with the UK, Australia and Brazil. In 2014, Russia set up a currency swap facility with the PBoC, the Chinese central bank. In the same year, a similar agreement was sign between the Swiss National Bank and PBoC up to a limit of CNY150 billion.[1] In same year, Sri Lanka government had signed CNY10 billion currency swap agreement with China. These efforts seem to help build a stable global market for trading the CNY. As a reserve foreign currency, in 2014, Australia has announced its intention of holding 5 %of reserves in CNY bonds, while Nigeria's central bank keeps at least 10 % of foreign exchange holdings in CNY.

In the trade clearing system, according to Deutsche Bank, in 2013, 17 % of China's trade was settled in CNY. Data from SWIFT,[2] the international currency clearing system, CNY is the fifth most used currency in the world for payments while investors are fast adding it to their trade. More than 2 % of world payments were conducted in CNY in December 2014. The CNY now sits the fifth behind the USD, euro, GBP and yen in terms of transactions.

In Recent years, foreign governments start to issue CNY denominated bonds. In October 2014, the UK has issued 2 billion government bonds denominated in CNY, the first time for the western country. Obviously, by issuing debt in CNY the UK is making a statement about its belief in the Chinese currency's future in the international monetary system. The UK Treasury Chancellor George Osborne explained, "...in order to increasing exports to fast-growing economies like China, it is indeed necessary ...to make sure, the CNY is used and traded here."[3] Also, the Canadian province of British Columbia has issued public bonds in late 2013. The Sri Lanka government is seriously examining proposal to issue a first CNY bond.

---

[1]"Grand global ambitions for renminbi sow domestic risks", *Financial Times*, 16th October, 2014.

[2]"Renminbi enters top five currencies for payments", *Financial Times*, 28th January 2015.

[3]Quoted from "UK takes first orders for debt renminbi bond", *Financial Times*, 15th October 2014.

2.1.3 *Structure and Characteristics of International Monetary System*

The international monetary system, a cooperative arrangement between sovereign nations, is composed of five main elements:

- a set of rules for setting exchange rates;
- a lender or lenders of last resort;
- instruments for providing liquidity and reserves (such as swap facilities among central banks and the special drawing right, an international reserve asset created by the IMF);
- provisions for surveillance;
- a reserve currency or currencies.

In practice, the core components of an international monetary system should contain the following three aspects:

- an international reserve standard played as an anchor in the system;
- arrangements such as an agreed foreign exchange regime to help adjust each participant's international balance of payment, and
- global collaboration mechanism.

The three aspects are crucial for defining and evaluating an international monetary system. When it comes to understand the past and the current international monetary system so as to find out the right approach for the future one, it is quite sensible for this book to focus on those three components.

As Salvatore (2011) point out, the main characteristics of the current IMS is, that there is a wide variety of exchange rate arrangements, nation is free to choose exchange rate regime, pegging or floating. Unlike previous systems—the pre-war gold standard and the Bretton Woods dollar standard, today's arrangement is characterised by the pronounced tendency of countries to tailor their exchange-rate regime to their own needs. Most importantly, countries decide whether to float or peg their currency, and to what currency or mix of currencies they should peg. They also choose what combination of currencies and gold to use as reserves. Because central banks want to hold reserves in currencies that are widely used in transactions, markets largely determine which currencies are used as reserves (Beattie 2011).

A minority of countries—68 of the 188 countries classified by the IMF—have chosen to float their currency. However, this group includes nearly all of the advanced economies and several of the large developing countries, such as Brazil, Mexico, India, and South Africa; together, the group accounts for almost 80 % of world GDP and 76 % of world trade. Thus, in terms of economic weight, today's exchange-rate system is overwhelmingly a floating system. About 120 countries choose to peg their currencies (or heavily manage them, according to the IMF classification). China stands out in this group. However, as Savona (2002, 2007) insisted, that based on the dual use (domestic and international) of the US dollar and the uncontrolled expansion of derivative markets, the free foreign exchange regime is dangerous to financial stability.

The international monetary system suffers from fundamental flaws, the Triffin dilemma and exclusion of emerging market. The Triffin Dilemma is referred where national or regional currencies to manage international liquidity. In other words, the inherent conflicts that arise when a national currency also serves as an international reserve currency and the system is unduly exposed to the vagaries of the so-called key reserve currency countries. In 1960, Robert Triffin (1960) noticed that holding dollars was more valuable than gold because constant U.S balance of payments deficits helped to keep the system liquid and fuel economic growth. What would later come to be known as Triffin's Dilemma was predicted when Triffin noted that if the U.S. failed to keep running deficits the system would lose its liquidity, not be able to keep up with the world's economic growth, and, thus, bring the system to a halt. But incurring such payment deficits also meant that, over time, the deficits would erode confidence in the dollar as the reserve currency created instability.

In order to solve the Triffin Dilemma, the alternative was handed out: paper gold. The existing gold stock could be "stretched" by issuing claims to purchasing power valued in terms of gold. As long as countries were willing to accept this "paper gold" at its face value, it would be used as reserves and exchanged at par with gold without changing its price. It would introduce a fiat component in the world money. Thus was born the Special Drawing Rights (SDRs), as the paper gold was called, and one unit was defined as the equivalent of one "1944" US dollar, i.e., 1/35th of an ounce of gold. Agreement on the SDRs was made at the 1967 Rio de Janeiro annual meeting of the IMF, and it was ratified, as the First Amendment to the Articles of Agreement of the IMF, in the following year. Each country would receive an "allocation," based on its quota in the Fund, and would be obliged to accept SDRs up to three times its allocation. After the Rio agreement there were great expectations not only that the SDRs would provide the needed supplement to the gold reserves but become the embryo of a genuine global currency.

By sketching the recently years'crisis and the development of world economy, the current IMS suffers from another fundamental flaw, saying the exclusion of emerging markets currencies. It implies that emerging markets, despite their increasing economic weight, remain mere bystanders of, rather than stakeholders in, the system and may therefore be less willing to align their policies with the stability of the system. Both aspects tilt the system inherently towards instability and external imbalances.

Clearly, problems in the international monetary system—persistent global imbalances, large and volatile capital flows, exchange rate gyrations disconnected from fundamentals, insufficient supply of safe global assets—are complex and call for an array of remedies—global policy collaboration and stronger surveillance, enhanced systemic financial safety net, financial deepening in emerging markets and more generally development of new reserve assets. The issue is whether there is a helpful role to play by reforming the IMS amid these solutions.

2.2 Proposals on Reforming the IMS Studies

The common wisdom is that an international agreement on a framework for financial sector reform should be arrived at. Maintaining central bank credibility as well as fiscal and regulatory credibility is essential to restore confidence to the IMS.

However, it is still not clear how to reform mechanism can impose adjustment on overcome the global imbalance. Furthermore, it is still quite arguable in which way to the IMS or smooth it to stabilize the global economy. The main arguments can be categorized into four strands:

2.2.1 *Maintaining the Status Quo of Dollar-Led International Monetary System*

Scholars (Subacchi and Driffill 2010; Meissner 2010; Dadush and Eidelman 2011) argued, although there are a lot weaknesses in the current international system, however, the dominant status of dollar is unreplaceable due to the reforming proposals (e.g. adding more weights for SDRs) of being far from satisfaction as well as the great political divergence remained between main states. They pointed out that the most important thing for the international monetary system is that the U.S and the Eurozone return to a sustainable and fiscally-sound growth path. Over a certain period of time, this will allow international interest rates to return to normal levels, alleviate fears of carry trades and hot-money inflows in emerging markets, and restore confidence in the main reserve currencies—precisely the changes needed to ensure that the international monetary system function smoothly.

Nakao (2010) argued, neither euro and yen, nor could CNY and SDRs become the global reserve currency or denominated currency. After all, the direction of reforming the IMS should be the stabilization of the current system by strengthening US dollar as anchor currency.

2.2.2 *Constructing CNY-Included Multi-Polar International Monetary System*

There are numerous works to promote the multi-polar international monetary system. Peng (2010) argued, that any monopoly international reserve monetary arrangement inherits intrinsic instability, the soaring of reserve pushes reverse mechanism to reform the international monetary system. All of the twin of deficit in U.S, low interest rate of dollar and expansion of dollar liquidity are inherited from the system dominated by dollar. They are balance measures by U.S, Unfortunately, it is knife-edged balance. This further develops Triffin dilemma. Meanwhile, the diversification of global economy challenges the existed international monetary system.

Mundell's work show the probability of improving the system advocated the practices of diversifying international money, among which the most representative one should be the Regional Monetary Cooperation based on the theory of Optimal Currency Area (OCA). The OCA theory stemmed from a debate about the relative merits between fixed exchange rate system and floating exchange rate system in 1960s. By that time, represented by Friedman (Friedman 1953), a group of economists believed that floating exchange rate system was the only effective measure to handling with the external shocks under the condition of rigid prices. On the other hand, Mundell (1961) diametrically pointed out that in the case of total and extensive application of the floating exchange rate, currency's function as monetary parity had no longer existed. The price anchor in global trade would also disappear so as to significantly increase the transaction cost in global trade and capital flow. On the basis of that and other academic contributions, Mundell proposed the OCA theory to illustrate the possibility of establishing an optimal currency area under a series of criteria and implementing a single currency as well as a fixed exchange rate system to protect the members from external shocks. His criteria were then supplemented by McKinnon (1969) and Kene (1969). The integration of the European Union had partly confirmed the theory in spite of a number of setbacks from practice. More importantly, the creation of the Euro and its subsequent performance in international monetary system had introduced another blueprint to fulfil the stability of the international monetary system. In the light of the road map of the Euro, an international monetary union would be established among several crucial international money such as the dollar, the Euro and the yen. These major international moneys would together play the role as international reserve currencies to avoid the excessive use of the dollar. Certainly, with the rise of the economic influence of China, the CNY has attracted more and more attention. In this respect, many economists are optimistic about the future role of the CNY in the diversified international currency system (Bergsten 2009; Eichengreen 2010; Jayakumar and Weiss 2011; Farhi, Gourinchas and Rey 2011).

Regarding to the internationalization of CNY, Bénassy-Quér and Pisani-Ferry (2011) argued, though the CNY is not yet convertible, the international monetary regime has already started to move towards a 'multipolar' system, with the dollar, the euro and the CNY as its key likely pillars. This shift corresponds to the long-term evolution of the balance of economic weight in the world economy. Such an evolution may mitigate some of the flaws of the present (non-) system, such as the rigidity of key exchange rates, the asymmetry of balance of-payments adjustments or what remains of the Triffin dilemma. However it may exacerbate other problems, such as short-run exchange rate volatility or the scope for 'currency wars', while leaving key questions unresolved, such as the response to capital flows global liquidity provision. Hence, in itself, a multipolar regime can be both the best and the worst of all regimes.

The basic advantage of a multi-polar reserve world is the concerns on transmission cost for replacing dollar as reserve currency (Krugman 1984). The second reason is, of course, that it provides space for diversification. As one stated, "if the dollar, the euro, and the CNY all have their problems, the very fact that there are doubts about all three is a reason to think that there will be a place for each of them" (Eichengreen 2010).

However,scholars (e.g. Stiglitz 2010) also argued that there are problems with a Multiple Currency Reserve System. They reckoned that a system based on multiple, competing reserve currencies would not resolve the difficulties associated with the current system. Under the multi-polar IMS,

> it would come at the cost of adding an additional element of instability: the exchange rate volatility among currencies used as reserve assets. If central banks and private agents were to respond to exchange rate fluctuations by changing the composition of their international assets, this would feed into exchange rate instability. Under these conditions, the response to the introduction of a multiple currency reserve system might be calls for a return to a fixed exchange rate arrangement." (Ibid., p. 165)

There have also been proposals to again give a greater role to gold (Zolick 2009). However, such a return to what Keynes called a 'barbarous relic' would be a non-starter. In particular, it would be inconsistent with the 'embedded liberalism' of earlier post-war arrangements—that the commitment to free markets is tempered by a broader commitment to social welfare and full employment (Eichengreen and Franke 1996).

2.2.3 Improving the Value and Allocation of SDRs

The SDRs might help serve respectively the following objectives: reducing the extent and costs of international reserve accumulation; augmenting the supply of safe global assets and facilitating diversification; and reducing the impact of exchange rate volatility among major currencies. Moghadam (2011) argued, expanding the SDRs basket to major emerging market currencies presents trade-offs, but could further support these objectives.

The SDRs has the features and potential to act as a super-sovereign reserve currency. Moreover, an increase in SDRs allocation would help the Fund address its resources problem and the difficulties in the voice and representation reform. Therefore, efforts should be made to push forward a SDRs allocation. Zhou Xiaochuan (2009) suggested, the desirable goal of reforming the international monetary system is to create an international reserve currency, saying SDRs. For the way of utilizing SDRs is disconnected from individual nations and is able to remain stable in the long run, thus removing the inherent deficiencies caused by using credit-based national currencies. Williamson (2009) also agreed that the most efficient way to improve the IMS is to enlarge the scale and functionality of SDRs.

Pisani-Ferry, Yu and Bénassy-Quéré (2011) argued that the most workable short-term deliverables seem to be (i) guidelines on and surveillance of capital controls; (ii) a new regime for deciding on SDRs allocations that would facilitate more frequent use of this instrument; and (iii) the inclusion of the CNY in the SDRs basket. These reforms would be a partial move, preparing the ground for further international monetary standard.

In order to manage the instabilities of a multicurrency system, a substitution account for allocating SDRs should be created in the IMF, to allow central banks to change their reserve composition without affecting markets (Kenen 2011).

To overcome problems of the current international monetary system, Ocampo (2014) proposed two reform routes: transforming it into a fully-fledged multicurrency reserve system or placing at the centre the only truly global reserve asset, the special drawing rights (SDRs). Mixing the two routes may be the only way forward. Under a mixed system, SDRs would become the source of financing for International Monetary Fund lending, but national/regional currencies would continue to be used as international means of payment and stores of value.

Contrary to above opinions, Farhi, Gourinchas and Rey (2011) argued, "their (SDRs) use -which can be justified under certain limited conditions—would not, in itself, cure the structural inefficiencies of the international monetary system.

2.2.4 Constructing a Supranational International Monetary System

It is not new to construct a supranational international monetary system. As the Keynes' proposal mentioned for creating an International Clearing Union or a similar solution offer, or to create a new international institution, a Global Reserve Bank (Stiglitz 2006; Chap. 9).

There are number of scholars suggested to introduce a global currency. Mundell called the major international money in current international monetary system, the Three Islands of Stability (G3) (Mundell 1995). He proposed that a new international monetary system would be finally established with a single supranational currency and a returned fixed exchange rate system. To achieve this goal, G3 should first reduce exchange rate volatility among them, and then gradually set their exchange rate system from a floating arrangement to a fixed one. Furthermore, Mundell (2011) reckoned that a similar to the introduction of euro, a dollar-euro as an anchor currency should be introduced. The exchange rate between dollar and euro remain fixed, other currencies can peg to the dollar-euro system.

Winkler (2010) argued the introduction of a super currency to manage the global liquidity as well as to manage the fluctuation of exchange rate. Gochoco-Bautista (2010) admitted to a super currency is a radical but effective way to deal with the cyclical capital flows and systematic risk in international monetary system.

In sum, the use of a dominant country-issued reserve currency such as the U.S dollar as an international reserve currency heightens the so-called Triffin dilemma. Theworld's demand for international reserve assets increases with international income and trade. The reserve-issuing country must continue to run balance of payments deficits to meet the growing demand, while surplus countries accumulate reserves, seemingly indefinitely (Bergsten 2009). The outstanding external debt of the reserve-issuing country would rise without limit, causing at some point investors to lose confidence in the value of reserve assets. There is no ready mechanism forcing surplus countries or the reserve-issuer to make an adjustment to fix the unsustainable systemic imbalance.

Reform of the international monetary system is under discussion after three decades of apathy. Tectonic shifts in the balance of international power have made reform more urgent. However, in the short term, there is little chance of a grand redesign of the international monetary system.

2.3 Research Question

By the end of the first decade of 21st century, a seemly sudden onset of constant defaults in housing industry in the US soon escalated into a banking turmoil. This contagion was quickly spread around the world through so-called financial innovations and finally drew most of the world into serious financial crisis and economic recession. The terrible crisis had pushed both the dollar and its backed system on the edge: the market confidence had been further weakened by the US' rounds of Quantitative Easing policy (QEs) and the "dollar glut" that flooded to every corner of the world had threaten the credibility of this de facto international standard. More importantly, this crisis had exposed structural problems of the current system and its frangibility.

Whereas it is argued that the huge imbalance continuously developed because of the different propensity to liquidity among major economies, which means too much credit on one side while savings glut on the other side. Monetary policies that oriented by domestic interest and the freedom to choose different exchange rate regime jointly make the current situation of global imbalance happened. Recent criticism about the manipulation of the exchange rate of CNY and the excessive use of Quantitative Easing of the dollar reflect this kind of opinions.

It is not surprised that in the era of post-Bretton Wood, especially most recently, neither the most sophisticated US dollar, nor the once powerful challenger the euro, and nor the seemly promising renminbi shows proper policy reactions to solve either their domestic monetary problems or international ones. On one hand, the traditional international liquidities, represented by the dollar and the euro, are suffering confidence crisis; while on the other hand, the renminbi is too premature to be an alternative one. As a consequence questions on the issue of international monetary standard arise.

In practice, the core components of an international monetary system should contain, among other things, the following three aspects: an international reserve standard played as an anchor in the system, some arrangements such as an agreed foreign exchange regime to help adjust each participant's international balance of payment, and accordingly global collaboration mechanism, like the practice from

G7/8 to G20. All the three aspects are crucial for defining and evaluating an international monetary system. When it comes to understand the past and the current international monetary system so as to find out the right approach for the future one, it is quite sensible for this book to focus on those three components.

This can be formulated as the following the model:

International Standards + Exchange Rate Regime + Coordinated Mechanism = IMS

However, the three elements are all worth carefully researching, thus cannot be all comprehensively included in one single book. Therefore, this book prepares to focus on one of them: International Standards.

The logical behind the research question is that, every crisis of International Monetary System is ultimately a crisis of the International Standards. From the Gold Standard, the Gold-exchange Standard, to the era of Paper Standard, it is acknowledged that the currency in the centre of IMS represents the nature of the system. Similarly, the current international monetary system crisis reflects the result of some internal flaws of the current international standard. This book tries to explore the future of international monetary system through the basic logic: how do the intrinsic flaws of the current international standards constrain their functions on prompting the IMS in a more sustainable and balanced way?

As the **Research Question**, this book is focused on [**different experiences of the current international standards, thus trying to understand what a sound international standard should be which is suitable for the future International Monetary System**].

2.3.1 Analytical Framework

Based on the model above, the research question can be further streamlined down into:

Q1 what are the performances of core currencies of current international monetary system?

Q2 comparing with all the forms of major currencies, what is a feasible way to establish a sound international monetary standard for the future international monetary system?

In this chapter and, Chaps. 3 and 4, I will focus on the current major moneys, the U.S. dollar, the euro and the CNY. As different experiences being a de facto international standard (or potentially), all the three could be grouped into: Sovereignty currency, Regional monetary integration and a Rising reserve currency. The chapters will first introduce the different monetary systems of the three, their monetary authorities and their performances on money supply. In the end of every chapter, the book tries to demonstrate the dilemma or the predicament they faced.

In the following Chapter of the book, it will put forward the performance of the existent standard of international monetary system, the SDRs. Equally, it will first introduce the characteristics of its monetary system and its trial for acting as a supranational international standard. Moreover in this section, the book tries to experiment the inclusion of China CNY to the current SDRs system, to see the potential changes the system would have, thus proposing the SDRs' new reform.

In the final section of the book, it intends to emphasize the background of the Bretton Woods system, so as to introducing the unsolved problems today for future research.

The analytical research is mainly based on comparing the performance of major international standards in the current international monetary system. Their political/policy reactions and economic philosophies behind them are not only, to some extent, the reasonable response to the current international monetary system, but also fundamental factors for deciding the forth coming changes or reforms of a future international monetary system.

2.3.2 Significance of the Work

The significance of the book is: firstly, from a perspective of international monetary system to analyse the different monetary systems of major international standards. Secondly, by comparing the major international standards, the book tries to understand how the preference in the domestic monetary policy influence the performances of major currencies as intentional standard. Thirdly, it tries to illustrate the appearance of CNY and its potential rising path. Ultimately, the purpose of studying on the book is to give rise to the question on how to put forward the feasible way to arrange a sound international monetary standard for the future international monetary system.

Chapter 3
Sovereign Dollar: "The Dollar Is Our Currency, but It's Your Problem"

In the past, gold had been long and widely adopted as a world monetary standard especially in the era rested on the conversion of paper notes into pre-set quantities of gold. Gold standard ensured the stability during most of commercial economy and the early stage of capitalism; however, it was confronted with embarrassment after unprecedented economic prosperity and waves of globalizations. The nature that helps it get the acknowledgement as a perfect standard, in turn, prevents it from long being. The limit quantity of gold was no longer suitable for the world's further prosperity. Therefore, another "ever-lasting" international standard, the paper money, was introduced firstly in modern time by Britain then followed the US dollar after the crash of the pound sterling. This new kind of standard was created in order to avoid the shortage of gold and was guaranteed by, at that time, the strongest economic and political sovereignty behind it.

The U.S. dollar had experience a rapid rising in the embers of World War II. It is without doubt that the whole Bretton Woods System had been founded on the basis of the U.S. dollar's role as the standard of international monetary system in post-war era. Despite times of "dollar shortage", this national currency standard served the world economy for decades while finally make a concession to its national interests of depreciation and freely floating. After that, the dollar-led international system goes on working till now under the "Washington Consensus".

Therefore, it is very necessary to have a closer look at the monetary system, the monetary authority, as well as the money supply in the U.S., say, the mechanism running behind the dollar.

3.1 Monetary System in the U.S

In spite of a complexly interplayed hierarchy system, monetary system in the U.S. establishes a comparatively independent monetary authority. It is the Federal Reserve that plays the role of the central bank as well as the money authority in effect in the country. Here we begin with the introduction of the structure of monetary system in the U.S., then focus on the monetary authority, the Fed and finally, we try to get an overview about the money supply in the U.S.

J. Wang, *The Past and Future of International Monetary System*,
SpringerBriefs in Economics, DOI 10.1007/978-981-10-0164-2_3

3.1.1 Structure of Monetary System in the U.S

The Federal Reserve System (also known as the Federal Reserve, and informally as the Fed) is the central banking system of the United States. Different from the People's Bank of China that operated as a department of the central government, the Fed is self-funded, with over 90 % of its revenues come from open market operations. More important, it is the central bank that is independent of government on monetary policy. As the State monetary authority, the Fed can make decisions on monetary affairs without the permission of Congress or the President even though its authority is derived from the U.S. Congress and is subject to congressional oversight. Moreover, even though the members of the Board of Governors, including its chairman and vice-chairman, are chosen by the President and confirmed by Congress.

Since it is a Federal Reserve System not just a single central bank, it owns a unique structure (see Graph 3.1). As a whole, the System holds the responsibility of the national central bank and subject to general Congressional authority and oversight but operates on its own earnings. In the center of the system, it has a Board of Governors to be the main governing body of the System. This Board is a federal agency, including seven members from wide range of industries appointed by the President and confirmed by the Senate. The governors of the Board own the rights to oversee System operations and to make regulatory decisions including setting reserve requirements.

Besides the Board, the Federal Open Market Committee (FOMC) is the most important monetary policymaking body of the Federal Reserve System. It consists of the 7 members of the Board and another 5 Reserve Bank presidents. Obviously, the Board of Governor constitutes a majority of the FOMC to make any key decisions on monetary policy. This Committee makes decisions regarding the conduct of open market operations which affect the provision of reserves to depository institutions and, in turn, the cost and availability of money and credit in the U.S. economy, as well as directs System operations in foreign currencies.

At the regional level, the whole State has been divided into twelve Federal Reserve Districts with totally 25 branches. Each district has a Federal Reserve Bank. All of them run as the operating arms of the State central banking system. Each is supervised by a board of nine directors who are divided into 3 classes, representing commercial banks in the districts (Class A) and consumers from various industries (Class B & C) respectively. All the Federal Reserve Banks share the responsibilities of carrying out Fed's daily operations on influencing the flow of money and credit in the nation's economy, initiating changes in the discount rate which is made by Reserve Banks to depository institutions at the "discount window", and monitoring the economy and financial institutions in their districts as well as providing financial services to the U.S. government and depository institutions.

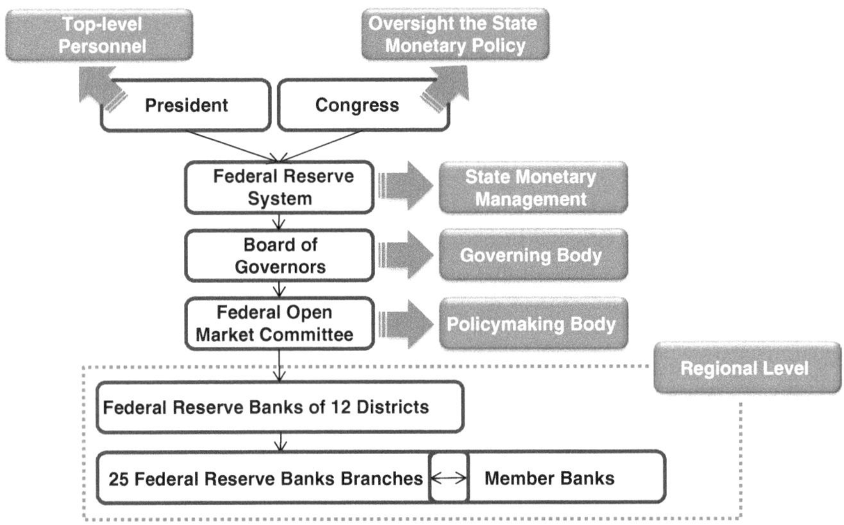

Graph 3.1 Structure of the federal reserve system

Under each Federal Reserve Bank, the system also has a number of member banks that hold stock in their local Federal Reserve Bank and operate as private banks.

In the unique monetary system, Fed has a decision-making process began with current situation and relative materials are provided for FOMC members and other Reserve Bank presidents, then there are reports from Manager of the FOMC on domestic open market and foreign currencies based on the current and prospective business situation, on conditions in financial markets, and on international financial developments. After that, considerations on prices and wages, employment and production, consumer income and spending, residential and commercial construction, business investment and inventories, foreign exchange markets, interest rates, money and credit aggregates, and fiscal policy are being taken and Committee must finally reach a consensus. Regarding the appropriate course for policy, which is incorporated in a directive to the Federal Reserve Bank of New York—the Bank that executes transactions for the System Open Market Account.

3.1.2 Monetary Authority and Its Performance in the U.S

(1) *Objectives of the Federal Reserve*

In its role as the central bank of the United States, the Fed serves as a banker's bank and as the government's bank. As the banker's bank, it helps to assure the safety and efficiency of the payments system. As the government's bank, or fiscal agent, the Fed processes a variety of financial transactions involving trillions of dollars. Just as an individual might keep an account at a bank, the U.S. Treasury keeps a checking account with the Federal Reserve through which incoming federal tax deposits and outgoing government payments are handled. As part of this service relationship, the Fed sells and redeems U.S. government securities such as savings bonds and Treasury bills, notes and bonds. It also issues the nation's coin and paper currency.

Its main objective today is to conduct the State monetary policy towards Full Employment, Stable Prices and Long-term Interest Rate Moderation so as to realize Promotion of Sustainable Economic Growth.

(2) *Main Responsibilities of the Federal Reserve*

Over time, the roles and responsibilities of the Federal Reserve System have expanded and its structure has evolved. The current functions of the Federal Reserve System are as followed.

Serve as the central bank for the United States, the Fed is responsible for managing the State money supply through monetary policy to achieve its objectives. Besides, the Fed supervises and regulates financial institutions in order to maintain the stability of the financial system and to contain systemic risk in financial markets. Finally, it has the responsibility of providing financial services to depository institutions, the U.S. government, and foreign official institutions, including playing a major role in operating the State payments system.

(3) *Main Instruments of the Monetary Policy in the U.S.*

The Fed has a toolbox of implementing the monetary policy. Open Market Operations, Federal Fund Rate and Discount Rate, as well as Reserve Requirements are among the most frequently used instruments.

Open market operations

Open market operations are the Federal Reserve's principal tool for implementing monetary policy through purchasing and selling of the U.S. Treasury and federal agency securities.

Federal funds rate and discount rate

The Fed implements monetary policy largely by targeting the federal funds rate. This is the rate that banks charge each other for overnight loans of federal funds, which are the reserves held by banks at the Fed. The Fed also directly sets the "discount rate", which the interest rate is charged to commercial banks and other depository institutions on loans they receive from their regional Federal Reserve Bank's lending facility–the discount window.

Reserve Requirements

Reserve requirements are the amount of funds set by the Fed that a depository institution must hold in reserve against specified deposit liabilities

(4) *Balance Sheet of Monetary Authority in the U.S.*

Besides a certain number of common items, the balance of Sheet in the world's biggest economy has its own characteristics (see Sheet 3.1).

Comparing with the items in the precious years, the Federal Reserve has implemented a number of changes with the items from 2013. In the sheet of 2015, there are Reserve Bank Credit, Foreign Currency Denominated Assets, Gold Stock, Special Drawing Rights Certificate Account and Treasury Currency Outstanding as the all channels that generate the assets of the Fed. Of which, the major one is definitely the channel of Reserve Bank Credit, which accounts for more than 98 % of total assets. It is mainly composed of securities held outright.

Securities held outright (93.24 %)
The securities held outright is the amount of securities held by Federal Reserve Banks and is controlled by open market operations. This quantity is the cumulative result of permanent open market operations: outright purchases or sales of securities, conducted by the Federal Reserve.

In this item, the U.S. Treasury securities accounts for a major part: it is the total face value of U.S. Treasury securities held by the Federal Reserve. This total is broken out as below:

- Bills are the current face value of the Federal Reserve's outright holdings of Treasury bills;
- Notes and bonds (nominal or inflation-indexed) are the current face value of the Federal Reserve's outright holdings of nominal or inflation-indexed Treasury notes and bonds;
- Inflation compensation reflects adjustments for the effects of inflation to the principal of inflation-indexed securities.

Besides are the Federal agency debt securities, which is the current face value of federal agency obligations held by Federal Reserve Banks (These securities are direct obligations of Fannie Mae, Freddie Mac, and the Federal Home Loan Banks) and the Mortgage-backed securities, which is the current face value of mortgage-backed obligations held by Federal Reserve Banks (These securities are guaranteed by Fannie Mae, Freddie Mac, or Ginnie Mae).

Repurchase agreements (Repos) and Discount loans (negligible amounts)
Repurchase agreements are transactions in which securities are purchased from a primary dealer under an agreement to sell them back to the dealer on a specified date in the future. It reflect some of the Federal Reserve's temporary open market operations. While the Loans is the sum of different kinds of loads, which could be broken out into Primary credit, Secondary credit, Seasonal credit, Term Asset-Backed Securities Loan Facility (TALF) as well as others.

Central bank liquidity swaps (negligible amounts)
The FOMC has authorized temporary reciprocal currency arrangements (central bank liquidity swaps) with certain foreign central banks to help provide liquidity in U.S. dollars to overseas markets.

Sheet 3.1 Official balance of sheet from monetary authority in the U.S (January, 2015)

Balance sheet of federal reserve on Jan 29, in 100 millions of dollars					
Assets		%	Liabilities		%
Reserve bank credit	44,687.49	98.18	Total factors, other than reserve balances, absorbing reserve funds	18,865.19	41.45
Securities held outright	42,439.67	93.24	Currency in circulation	13,289.75	29.20
U.S. Treasury securities	24,608.56	54.06	Reverse repurchase agreements	2574.82	5.66
Bills	0.00	0.00	Foreign official and international accounts	1159.65	2.55
Notes and bonds, nominal	23,467.12	51.56	Others	1415.17	3.11
Notes and bonds, inflation-indexed	984.69	2.16	Treasury cash holdings	2.16	0.00
Inflation compensation	156.75	0.34	Deposits with F.R. banks, other than reserve balances	2374.55	5.22
Federal agency debt securities	375.88	0.83	Term deposits held by depository institutions	0.00	0.00
Mortgage-backed securities	17,455.24	38.35	U.S. treasury, general account	2011.92	4.42
Unamortized premiums on securities held outright	2,060.79	4.53	Foreign official	52.30	0.11
Unamortized discounts on securities held outright	−182.73	−0.40	Other	310.33	0.68
Repurchase agreements	0.00	0.00	Other liabilities and capital	623.91	1.37
Loans	0.39	0.00	Reserve balances with federal reserve banks	26,651.53	58.55
Primary credit	0.31	0.00			
Secondary credit	0.00	0.00			
Seasonal credit	0.09	0.00			
Term asset-backed securities loan Facility	0.00	0.00			

(continued)

Sheet 3.1 (continued)

Balance sheet of federal reserve on Jan 29, in 100 millions of dollars					
Assets		%	Liabilities		%
Other credit extensions	0.00	0.00			
Net portfolio holdings of Maiden Lane LLC	16.81	0.04			
Net portfolio holdings of Maiden Lane II LLC	0.00	0.00			
Net portfolio holdings of Maiden Lane III LLC	0.00	0.00			
Net portfolio holdings of TALF LLC	0.00	0.00			
Float	−3.67	−0.01			
Central bank liquidity swaps	0.02	0.00			
Other federal reserve assets	356.19	0.78			
Foreign currency denominated assets	202.72	0.45			
Gold stock	110.41	0.24			
Special drawing rights certificate account	52.00	0.11			
Treasury currency outstanding	464.11	1.02			
Total factors supplying reserve funds	45516.72	100.00	Total factor absorbing reserve funds	45,516.72	100.00

Foreign currency denominated assets (0.45 %)
Foreign currencies are revalued daily to reflect movements in market exchange rates each day.

Gold stock (0.24 %)
The gold stock of the United States is held by the Treasury and consists of gold that has been monetized: the Treasury has issued certificates reflecting the value of the gold to the Federal Reserve in return for a credit for the same dollar value to the Treasury's accounts.

Special drawing rights certificate account (0.11 %)
Under the law providing for the United States' participation in the SDRs system, the Secretary of the Treasury is authorized to issue SDRs certificates, somewhat similar to gold certificates, to the Reserve Banks, which are required to purchase the SDRs for the purpose of financing SDRs acquisitions or exchange stabilization operations. The value of the SDRs is established monthly, based on the exchange rates of a number of the underlying currencies.

Treasury currency outstanding (1.02 %)
Coin and paper currency (excluding Federal Reserve notes) held by the public, financial institutions, Reserve Banks, and the Treasury are liabilities of the U.S. Treasury. This item consists primarily of coin, but includes about a small amount of U.S. notes–that is, liabilities of the U.S. Treasury–that have been outstanding since the late 1970s. U.S. notes are no longer issued.

On the side of liabilities, there are also some changes in the sheet of 2015. The items in this side represent factors that are responsible for absorbing the reserve funds, which can be divided into two groups. One is Reserve Balance with Federal Reserve Banks, the other one is composed of total factors that other than the first one.

Total Factors, Other Than Reserve Balances, Absorbing Reserve Funds (41.45 %)
This total is mainly broken out as below:

- Currency in circulation includes paper currency and coin held both by the public and in the vaults of depository institutions. The total includes Treasury estimates of coins outstanding and Treasury paper currency outstanding (This definition of currency in circulation differs from the currency component of the money stock, which excludes currency held in vaults of depository institutions).
- Reverse repurchase agreements are transactions in which securities are sold to a set of counterparties under an agreement to buy them back from the same party on a specified date at the same price plus interest. It may be conducted with foreign official and international accounts as a service to the holders of these accounts.
- Treasury cash holdings include paper currency and coin held in Treasury vaults, including silver bullion, silver dollars, coinage metal, and unmonetized gold. The value of Treasury cash holdings is estimated using Treasury data.
- Deposits with F.R. Banks, other than reserve balances are the sum of "Term deposits held by depository institutions," "U.S. Treasury, General Account," "U.S. Treasury, Supplementary Financing Account," "Foreign official accounts," and "Other deposits." They are separate and distinct from balances maintained in an institution's master account at a Federal Reserve Bank as well as from those maintained in an excess balance account. Some of them are intended to facilitate the conduct of monetary policy by providing a tool for managing the aggregate quantity of reserve balances.

Reserves Balances (58.55 %)
Reserve balances with Federal Reserve Banks are the difference between "total factors supplying reserve funds" and "total factors, other than reserve balances, absorbing reserve funds." This item includes balances at the Fcdcral Rcscrvc of all depository institutions that are used to satisfy reserve requirements (required reserves) and balances held in excess of balance requirements (excess reserves). It excludes reserves held in the form of cash in bank vaults.

The balance sheet of a monetary authority usually brings us with "a pair of lenses" to understand easier and more clearly about the complex monetary phenomenon of a state. By reading this sheet of a central bank, we can get the knowledge of State money issuing regime, different channels that creating the money resources and all the factors that absorbing them, on the other side. From the figures of the sheet, we can get the amount of aggregate demand of money in a period of time and find out how they could be injected into the economy. Evermore, we can use some formula, such as the money multiplier, to calculate the ability of money creation in a state bank system so as to gain further economic meanings.

Comparison with the balance sheet of states is of significant to realize the different levels of monetary system efficiencies and thereby to understand the different degrees of their economic vulnerabilities against any changes.

From the Assets side, we classified all the factors that providing the base money into three "channels". They are named as "Base Money Foreign", "Base Money Treasury" and "Base Money Banks". Therefore, the sheet can be simplified on the basis of different groups. money in the U.S. On the Liabilities side, besides "Currency Issue" and "Reserve Requirement" that constitute the "Reserve Money", there are "Bank Factors," "Foreign Factors," "Treasury Factors" and other liabilities and capital that are responsible for absorbing the reserve funds. (see Sheet 3.2).

In this simplified balance sheet of monetary authority in the U.S., we group "Securities held outright" and "Treasury currency outstanding" as "Base Money Treasury"; group "Foreign currency denominated assets," "Gold Stock" and "Special drawing rights certificate account" as "Base Money Foreign"; name "Central bank liquidity swaps," "Float" and " Other Federal Reserve assets" as "Other Assets"; and group all the rest items as "Base Money Bank". Similarly, on the side of Liabilities, "Treasury cash holdings" and "U.S. Treasury, General Account" could be grouped as "Treasury Factors"; "Foreign official and international accounts" and "Foreign official" as "Foreign Factors"; "Others" in "Reverse repurchase agreements" and in "Deposits with F.R. Banks, other than reserve balances", as well as "Term deposits held by depository institutions" could be described as "Bank Factors"; there are also "Other Liabilities and Capitals".

From this simplified edition, it is clear that the largest source of Base Money in the U.S. is through the Treasury channel, which is up to 94 %. Followed by Bank channel (4.16 %). It is noted that the Fed has very marginal Foreign Exchange reserves and it has no need to hold them actually.

Meanwhile, apart from Currency in Circulation (29.2 %), Reserve Requirement, which is composed of Compulsory and Excess ones constitutes more than half of

Sheet 3.2 Simplified balance of sheet (January, 2015)

Simplified balance sheet of monetary authority in the U.S. on Jan 29, in 100 millions of dollars					
Assets		%	Liabilities		%
Base money foreign	365.13	0.80	Currency issue (currency in circulation)	13,289.75	29.20
Base money treasury	42,903.78	94.26	Reserve requirement (compulsory and excess)	26,651.53	58.55
Base money banks	1895.66	4.16	Bank factors	1725.50	3.79
Other assets	352.54	0.77	Foreign factors	1211.95	2.66
			Treasury factors	2014.08	4.42
			Other liabilities and capital	623.91	1.37
Total assets	45,516.72	100.00	Total liabilities	45,516.72	100.00

Fed's Liabilities (58.55 %). Others, say Treasury Factors, Foreign Factors as well as Bank Factors are all marginal in the process of sterilization.

3.1.3 Monetary Supply in the U.S

Sheet 3.3 outlines the key indicators of money aggregates in the U.S. from 2006 to 2014. From these data, we could observe the features of monetary supply in the U.S.

In the U.S.,

- Monetary Base = Currency in Circulation + Reserve Requirement = Currency in Circulation + (Required Reserves + Excess Reserves);
- Money Supply = (Money Multiplier) * (Monetary Base);
- *If*,

M0 = Currency in Circulation, MS = Money Supply = M2,[1] *m = Money Multiplier, B = Base Money*

$MS = m * B \rightarrow M2 = m * B \rightarrow m = M2/B$[2]

Also in Sheet 3.3, we can calculate the Money Multiplier in the U.S. from 2006 to 2014 directly using M2/Base Money.[3]

[1]We use the data of M2 as all forms of deposits in financial system.

[2]We get Currency in Circulation (M0), M2 and Base Money (Monetary Base) from the official reports.

[3]Money Multiplier announced by the official reports is almost the same as the Money Multiplier that calculated directly using M2/Base Money, except some certain quarters.

Sheet 3.3 Money Supply and money multiplier in the U.S

U.S. in billion dollar	2006 Q1	2006 Q2	2006 Q3	2006 Q4	2007 Q1	2007 Q2	2007 Q3	2007 Q4	2008 Q1	2008 Q2	2008 Q3	2008 Q4
M0 = currency in circulation	789	795	794	811	806	812	812	822	816	824	835	878
M2 = money supply	6753	6835	6928	7066	7154	7270	7402	7495	7676	7745	7892	8248
Monetary base	810	812	810	827	821	827	827	837	833	840	910	1666
Money multiplier	8.34	8.41	8.55	8.55	8.71	8.79	8.95	8.95	9.21	9.22	8.68	4.95
U.S. in billion dollar	2009 Q1	2009 Q2	2009 Q3	2009 Q4	2010 Q1	2010 Q2	2010 Q3	2010 Q4	2011 Q1	2011 Q2	2011 Q3	2011 Q4
M0 = currency in circulation	901	908	913	924	933	941	952	980	1002	1024	1038	1067
M2 = money supply	8402	8455	8454	8531	8512	8591	8700	8812	8926	9094	9478	9639
Monetary base	1647	1684	1801	2026	2080	2002	1961	2017	2395	2649	2638	2620
Money multiplier	5.10	5.02	4.69	4.21	4.09	4.29	4.44	4.37	3.73	3.43	3.59	3.68
U.S. in billion dollar	2012 Q1	2012 Q2	2012 Q3	2012 Q4	2013 Q1	2013 Q2	2013 Q3	2013 Q4	2014 Q1	2014 Q2	2014 Q3	2014 Q4
M0 = currency in circulation	1095	1109	1126	1159	1175	1191	1206	1232	1263	1280	1290	1328
M2 = money supply	9785	9922	10,169	10,417	10,484	10,639	10,802	10,975	11,173	11,343	11,474	11,626
Monetary base	2655	2619	2595	2676	2935	3201	3487	3717	3886	3949	4049	3934
Money multiplier	3.69	3.79	3.92	3.89	3.57	3.32	3.10	2.95	2.88	2.87	2.83	2.95

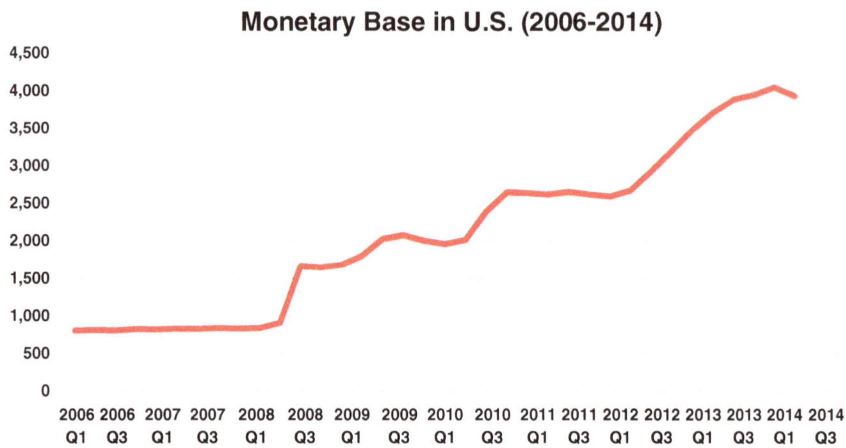

Graph 3.2 Changes of monetary base in the U.S. (2006–2014)

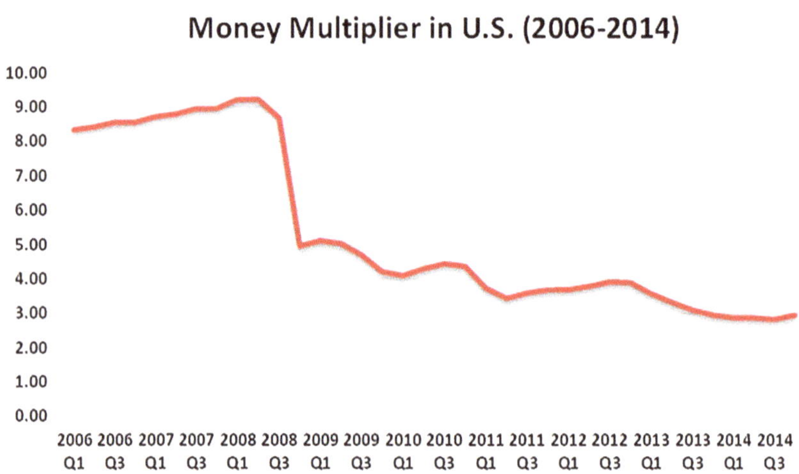

Graph 3.3 Changes of money multiplier in the U.S. (2006–2014)

Here are the graphs from which we can directly observe the changes of monetary base and money multipliers in the U.S. in the recent years. (See Graphs 3.2, 3.3, 3.4, 3.5)

Apparently, there are two phrases in the period: before the Financial Crisis, the monetary base in the U.S. was steady while after that, the curve was rising sharply, from 910 billion dollars in 2008 Q3 soaring to 1,666 billion dollars in 2008 Q4. On the contrary, in the Graph of Changes of Money Multiplier in the U.S. (Graph 3.3), there has been a reverse change in the same phrase: after the Financial Crisis, the

Money Multiplier was sharply going downside from 8.68 in 2008 Q3 to 4.95 in 2008 Q4.

Although money multiplier was usually described to be the accelerator of the economy, this turnaround during the Financial Crisis could be a result of the economic recession in the U.S.

Additionally we broke Monetary Base down into its two elements, "Currency in Circulation" and "Reserve Requirement" (See Graphs 3.4 and 3.5). The shadow area of the two graphs represent the period of Economic Recession in the U.S. by the Fed. Now we all have the idea that the prominent increasement in the shadow area of both "Currency in Circulation" and "Reserve Requirement" were the reflection of the famous "Quantitative Easing". From then on, all these unorthodox policies have ballooned the Fed's balance sheet.

3.2 "The Dollar Is Our Currency, but It's Your Problem"

As we all known, the Bretton Woods system became operational in 1946, with key features including fixing the US dollar to the price of gold at $35 an ounce and having other countries maintain a fixed and agreed parity vis-à-vis the dollar, e.g., gold. The unravelling reached a tipping point in 1970 when the US economy was suffering from a host of ills: inflation approaching 6 %, GDP growth south of 1 %, an emerging CA deficit, and gold coverage falling from 55 to 22 %. Soon after came President Richard Nixon's justifiably infamous "new economic policy",

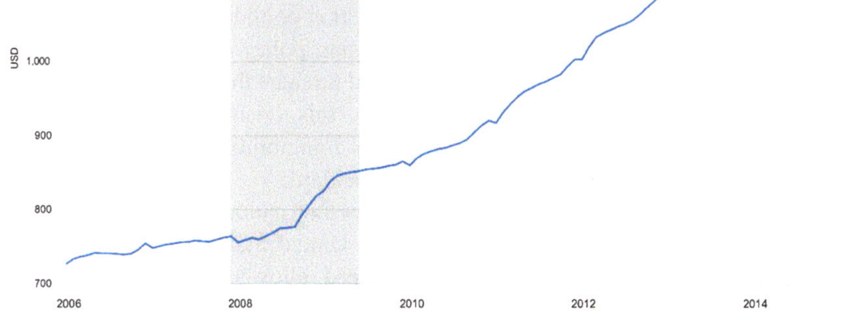

Graph 3.4 Changes of currency in circulation in the U.S. (2006–2014)

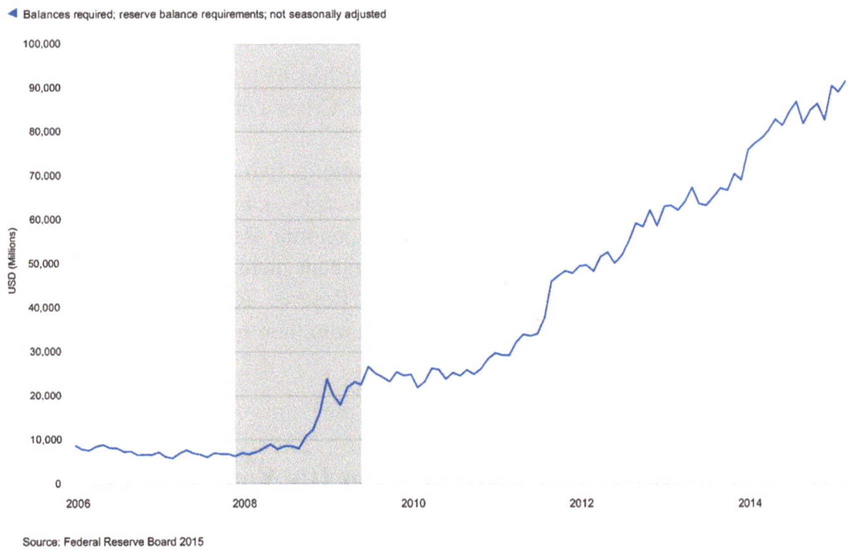

Graph 3.5 Changes of reserve requirement in the U.S. (2006–2014)

announced on 15 August 1971. The prime architect of the "Nixon shock" was Treasury Secretary John Connally and included a brazenly unilateral 10 % surcharge on all dutiable imports, a 10 % reduction in foreign assistance expenditures, 90-day wage and price controls, as well as closing the "gold window" (so the dollar was no longer freely convertible). Then, came the intended consequence of driving yet another nail into the coffin of Bretton Woods and leading in short order to a roughly 20 % depreciation of the dollar.

More recently, by the end of the first decade of new millennium, a seemly sudden onset of constant defaults in housing industry in the US soon escalated into a banking turmoil. This contagion was quickly spread around the world through so-called financial innovations and finally drew most of the world into serious financial crisis and economic recession. The terrible crisis had pushed both the dollar and its backed system on the edge: the market confidence had been further weakened by the US' rounds of Quantitative Easing policy (QEs) and the "dollar glut" that flooded to every corner of the world had threaten the credibility of this de facto international standard. More importantly, this crisis had again exposed structural problems of the current system and its frangibility: too dependent on a sovereign dollar as the international monetary standard.

The design of the Bretton Woods System was that nations could only enforce gold convertibility on the anchor currency—the United States' dollar. Gold convertibility enforcement was not required, but instead, allowed. Nations could forgo converting dollars to gold, and instead hold dollars. Rather than full convertibility, it provided a fixed price for sales between central banks. However, there was still an open gold market. For the Bretton Woods system to remain workable, it would either have to alter the peg of the dollar to gold, or it would have to maintain the free market price for gold near the $35 per ounce official price. The greater the gap between free market gold prices and central bank gold prices, the greater the temptation to deal with internal economic issues by buying gold at the Bretton Woods price and selling it on the open market. In 1960 Robert Triffin, Belgian American economist, noticed that holding dollars was more valuable than gold because constant U.S. balance of payments deficits helped to keep the system liquid and fuel economic growth. What would later come to be known as Triffin's Dilemma was predicted when Triffin noted that if the U.S. failed to keep running deficits the system would lose its liquidity, not be able to keep up with the world's economic growth, and, thus, bring the system to a halt. But incurring such payment deficits also meant that, over time, the deficits would erode confidence in the dollar as the reserve currency created instability.

Despite of the internal structural dilemma, the state quo of the U.S. dollar as an international monetary standard also made it possible to own other "special benefits".

International Seigniorage

Over the past decade there has been considerable controversy concerning the amount of U.S. currency circulating abroad. Porter and Judson have claimed that in the mid-nineties between 53–67 % of U.S. currency was overseas, whereas Feige's estimates suggested a figure closer to 40 % abroad. Most recently, Goldberg writing in a New York Federal Reserve publication asserted that "about 65 % ($580 billion) of all banknotes are in circulation outside of the country". However, these assertions are contradicted by the Federal Reserve Board of Governors Flow of Funds statistics which show that at the end of March 2009, only $313 billion (36.7 %) of U.S. currency was held abroad. Feige calculates that since 1964, "the cumulative seigniorage earnings accruing to the U.S. by virtue of the currency held by foreigners amounted to $167–$185 billion and over the past two decades seigniorage revenues from foreigners have averaged $6–$7 billion dollars per year".

Exorbitant Privilege

The term exorbitant privilege[4] specifically refers to the alleged benefit the U.S. has due to its own currency being the international reserve currency. Accordingly, the US would not face a balance of payments crisis, because it purchased imports in its own currency. In simple words, the U.S. is able to consume on debt without consideration of the situation of national balance of payments

The Possible Trinity

[4]Academically, the exorbitant privilege literature analyses two empiric puzzles, the position and the income puzzle. The position puzzle consists of the difference between the (negative) U.S. net international investment position (NIIP) and the accumulated U.S. current account deficits, the former being much smaller than the latter. The income puzzle consists of the fact that despite a deeply negative NIIP, the U.S. income balance is positive, i.e. despite having much more liabilities than assets, earned income is higher than interest expenses.

According to the impossible trinity, a central bank can only pursue two of the above-mentioned three policies simultaneously. Hence, all three of the policy objectives mentioned above cannot be pursued simultaneously. A central bank has to forgo one of the three objectives. Therefore a central bank has three policy combination options: (a) Stable Exchange Rate and Free Capital Flow, (b) Independent Monetary Policy and Free Capital Flow, (c) Stable Exchange Rate and Independent Monetary Policy. However, in the U.S., there is no restrictions above. From the study of the U.S.' monetary system and the process of its money supply, the Fed implements monetary policy solely depending on the national interests. Moreover, it is without any doubts that the U.S. owns the most freedom and the most active capital markets in the world. As for the stable exchange rate, though the dollar applies floating exchange regime, more than 50 nations in the world implement the dollar-pegged regime, which in turn shows the de facto "fixed exchange regime" the dollar possessed in the international economic activities. All to all, there are great degree of independence for U.S. monetary policy that could escaped from the restrictions of "The Impossible Trinity".[5]

It is reminded that at the G-10 Rome meetings held in late 1971, the U.S. Treasury Secretary Connally proclaimed to his astonished counterparts, "The dollar is our currency, but it's your problem,"

[5]The Impossible Trinity (also known as the Trilemma) is a trilemma in international economics which states that it is impossible to have all three of the following at the same time: A stable foreign exchange rate, Free capital movement (absence of capital controls), and An independent monetary policy.

Chapter 4
Regional Euro: "Creative, Ambitious, but Trapped"

From its very beginning, the euro has been an important international currency and is bound to become even more so in the future. In other words, the creation of the euro had been regarded as a creative challenger to the international dollar standard, which was full of ambitions. There were some reasons by that time: the European Monetary Union (EMU) was almost as huge an economic and trading unit as the U.S.; it had a large, well-developed and growing financial market, which was increasingly free and was expected to have a good inflation performance that will keep the value of the euro stable.

More importantly, the experiment of euro represented an idea for a world currency. As Robert Mundell pointed out, a world currency would level the playing field for big and small economies alike. Realizing that this is not likely to occur in the foreseeable future, scholars shared this view opted for the second best solution of returning to a fixed exchange rate system "a la Bretton Woods", but with countries not sterilizing changes in their money supply resulting from balance of payments disequilibria.

As a first step in this direction, the euro was designed and introduced as a regional currency. Therefore, it is certainly important to understand the running system of the regional currency, including its structure, its central bank, as well as its money supply.

4.1 Monetary System in the Eurozone

The Monetary System in the Eurozone reflects collective actions of European Union member states that have adopted the euro as their sole official currency. Politically, there is two-layer structure in the system, and is distinct from the European System of Central Banks, which is the group of central banks. From this perspective, it could be creative.

J. Wang, *The Past and Future of International Monetary System*,
SpringerBriefs in Economics, DOI 10.1007/978-981-10-0164-2_4

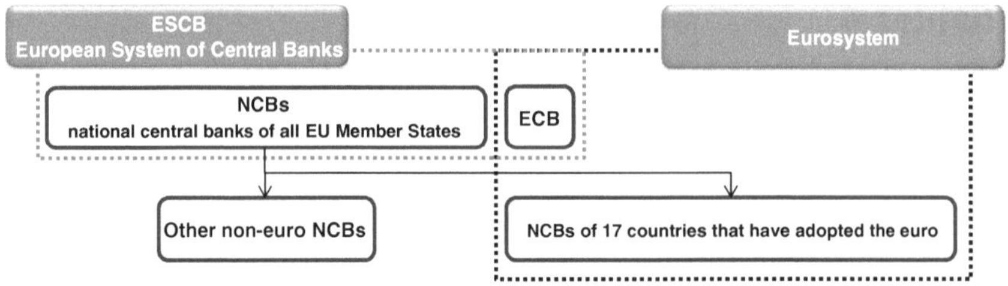

Graph 4.1 Structure of the Eurozone

4.1.1 *The Structure of the Monetary Authority in the Eurozone*

Before looking at the structure of the monetary authority in the Eurozone, there are some similar terms that need to be defined.

Since 1st January 1999 the European Central Bank (ECB) has been responsible for defining, implementing and conducting monetary policy for the euro area. According to the unique organization of the European Union, not all member states of the Union have joined the single currency area, the Eurozone. Accordingly, other unique systems should be established to make sure the necessary collaborative work could be done (see Graph 4.1).

Therefore, the Eurosystem was created to comprise the ECB and the NCBs of 17 countries that have adopted the euro is the monetary authority of the euro area, of which, Austria, Belgium, Finland, France, Germany, Ireland, Italy, Luxemburg, Netherlands, Portugal and Spain are the early group, followed Greece, Slovenia, Cyprus, Malta, Slovakia and Estonia. Meanwhile, to be better understood and better implemented with the Union, another European System of Central Banks (ESCB) is needed to comprise the ECB and the national central banks (NCBs) of all EU Member States whether they have adopted the euro or not.

According to Article 282, the Treaty on the Functioning of the European Union, in the center of the network, "the European Central Bank, together with the national central banks of the Member States whose currency is the euro, which constitute the Eurosystem, shall conduct the monetary policy of the Union." Also acknowledged by the Treaty, "the primary objective of the Eurosystem shall be to maintain price stability[1]". The aim defined by the ECB is to maintain inflation rates at levels below, but close to, 2 % over the medium term. Under the primary aim, the Eurosystem takes monetary policy decisions based on an overall assessment of the

[1]It was clarified by the Governing Council of the ECB in October 1998 that "price stability shall be defined as a year-on-year increase in the Harmonised Index of Consumer Prices (HICP) for the euro area of below 2 %. Price stability is to be maintained over the medium term".

risks to price stability. This kind of assessment can be divided into Economic Analysis and Monetary Analysis that cross-checked with each other.

Meanwhile, Article 130 emphasizes "when exercising the powers and carrying out the tasks and duties conferred upon them by the Treaties and the Statute of the ESCB and of the ECB..., neither the ECB, nor a national central bank, nor any member of their decision-making bodies shall seek or take instructions from Union institutions, bodies, offices or agencies, from any government of a Member State or from any other body." These articles give the core monetary management body—the European Central Bank a firm, legal foundation and a necessary extent of independence.

4.1.2 Monetary Authority and Its Performance in the Eurosystem

Within the European Central Bank, it has a Governing Council which is the main decision-making body consisting of the six members of the Executive Board, plus the governors of the NCBs of the 17 euro area countries. This body is responsible for "adopting guidelines and decisions to ensure the performance of the tasks of the Eurosystem," formulating monetary policy for the euro area. The Executive Board that consists of the President, Vice-President and four other members who are appointed by the European Council, acts by a qualified majority and is responsible for implementing monetary policy for the euro area in accordance with the guidelines specified and decisions taken by the Governing Council, including giving the necessary instructions to the euro area NCBs and exercising regulatory powers delegated to it by the Governing Council. Besides these, there is a General Council that comprises the President and the Vice-President of the ECB, and the governors of the NCBs of the 27 EU Member States (other members of the ECB's Executive Board, the President of the EU Council and one member of the European Commission may attend the meetings of the General Council but do not have the right to vote). It is a council that can be regarded as a transitional body before all EU member states applying the euro. Moreover, it is responsible for the ECB's advisory functions, establishes the necessary rules for standardizing the accounting and reporting of operations undertaken by the NCBs, prepares for irrevocably fixing the exchange rates of the currencies of the "EU Member States with a derogation" against the euro.

(1) *Objectives of the ECB*

In accordance with the Eurosystem, the objective of the ECB is to maintain price stability: safeguarding the value of the euro.

(2) *Main Responsibilities of the ECB*

Under the guidelines and instructions either conferred by the Treaty or delegated by EU Council, the European Central Bank holds the responsibility to the definition of the Eurosystem policies as well as the responsibility to decide, coordinate and monitor the monetary operations including strategic planning about the amount of liquidity, and over sighting, or even intervening when it is necessary, of the financial market and payment instruments in the Eurozone. It also plays the advisory functions to Community institutions and national authorities.

For the unique structure of the monetary authority in the Eurozone and to be better understood and deeply cooperated, the ECB should also prepare to have recourse to the national central banks to carry out operations if possible and appropriate.

(3) *Main Instruments of the Monetary Policy in the Eurozone*

The main and standard monetary instruments applied by the ECB include Standing Facilities, Open Market Operations and Reserve Requirements.

Standing facilities
This kind of instruments provides a ceiling and a floor for the overnight rate in the money market. It contains Deposit Facility and Marginal Lending Facilities. Deposit Facility, which can be used by counterparties to make overnight deposits with the national central banks, also enjoy a rate generally lower than the market rates. However, Marginal Lending Facility, which allows counterparties to obtain overnight liquidity from the national central banks against eligible assets, is often with a higher rate.

Open market operations This category represents the most important instrument for the monetary policy, which could be described as a group of Refinancing Operations. The ECB assesses the total liquidity need of the banking sector and, in competitive tenders, allots this amount. Usually these tenders are conducted as variable rate tenders, meaning that banks pay the interest that they offer when they make their bids. The ECB may also execute its tenders in the form of fixed rate tenders, where the interest rate is specified in advance and banks bid the amount of money they wish to transact at the fixed interest rate. The whole process is called Refinancing Operations. To distinguish their own differences, there are four kind of refinancing operations: Main Refinancing Operations, followed by Longer-term Refinancing Operations, Fine-tuning Operations and Structural Operations.

Main Refinancing Operations are regular liquidity-providing reverse transactions usually with a weekly frequency and a maturity of one week. While Longer-term Refinancing Operations are with a monthly frequency and a maturity of, normally, three months; in exceptional circumstances, the ECB can increase the frequency and the maturity of these operations. Compare to these two, another two are more or less contemporary ones: Fine-tuning Operations are executed on an ad hoc basis and Structural Operations are executed whenever the ECB wishes to adjust the structural liquidity position of the Eurosystem.

Reserve Requirements
ECB requires credit institutions to hold minimum reserves on accounts with the national central banks. Generally, 2 % is the reserve ratio for the majority of the items to which the reserves base applies. On the other side, the reserve holdings will be remunerated at the Eurosystem's rate on its Main Refinancing Operations.

Non-Standard Measures
In order to provide a high degree of flexibility to counter unforeseen situations and aimed at the banking sector given the reliance of companies on financing by banks (as opposed to financing via capital markets), the ECB also equips a number of non-standard measures. Firstly, ECB may decide in advance to allot the full amount of liquidity that banks request, i.e. to accommodate all bids, at a fixed interest rate, which is called Fixed-rate, Full-allotment Liquidity Provision. Secondly, Expansion of List of Assets Eligible as Collateral means that the ECB can decide to lower the minimum requirements for collateral that banks have to provide when they borrow money from the Eurosystem. If there is a problem in the banks' access to liquidity in foreign currencies, the ECB can provide this liquidity called Liquidity Provision in Foreign Currencies and Foreign Exchange Swap Operations in cooperation with other central banks.[2] The fourth one is Outright Purchases of Covered Bonds (or some specific debt securities) which is designed to support certain market segments. Actually, Eurosystem can, instead of just accepting certain assets as collateral, decide to purchase certain assets directly.[3]

Eurosystem may conduct interventions in the euro area's public and private debt securities markets through Securities Markets Programme (SMP) which is supposed to ensure the proper transmission of monetary policy impulses to the wider economy and, ultimately, to the general price level.

(4) *Balance Sheet of Monetary Authority in the Eurosystem*

The balance sheet of monetary authority in the Eurosystem is called the Consolidated Financial Statement of the Eurosystem (see Sheet 4.1).

From the Assets side, the item Securities of Euro Area Residents in Euro and Lending to Euro Area Credit Institutions in Euro are among the most, being 27.65 and 26.57 % respectively. Then comes the item Gold and Gold Receivables

[2]The euro liquidity absorption resulting from the provision of foreign currency to Eurosystem counter parties via FX swaps was discontinued in January 2010. Until June 2009, this euro liquidity absorption was displayed under autonomous factors, while thereafter is has been part of outstanding open market operations.

[3]Covered bond portfolio is displayed under open market operations. The Eurosystem's Covered Bond Purchase Programme ended, as planned, on 30 June 2010 when it reached a nominal amount of €60 billion. The Eurosystem intends to hold the assets bought under this programme until maturity.

Sheet 4.1 Balance of sheet from monetary authority in the Eurosystem (January, 2015)

Consolidated Financial Statement of the Eurosystem (EUR Millions, January 2015)					
Assets	Amount	%	Liabilities	Amount	%
Gold and gold receivables	343,867.00	15.76	Banknotes in circulation	1,004,230.00	46.02
Claims on non-euro area residents in foreign currency	273,726.00	12.54	Liabilities to euro area credit institutions in euro	264,523.00	12.12
Claims on euro area residents in foreign currency	35,549.00	1.63	Current accounts (covering the minimum reserve system)	227,385.00	10.42
Claims on non-euro area residents in euro	18,597.00	0.85	Deposit facility	36,557.00	1.68
Lending to euro area credit institutions in euro	579,646.00	26.57	Fixed-term deposits	0.00	0.00
Main refinancing operations	163,821.00	7.51	Fine-tuning reverse operations	0.00	0.00
Longer-term refinancing operations	415,608.00	19.05	Deposits related to margin calls	581.00	0.03
Fine-tuning reverse operations	0.00	0.00	Other liabilities to euro area credit institutions in euro	5556.00	0.25
Structural reverse operations	0.00	0.00	Debt certificates issued	0.00	0.00
Marginal lending facility	217.00	0.01	Liabilities to other euro area residents in euro	111,448.00	5.11
Credits related to margin calls	0.00	0.00	Liabilities to non-euro area residents in euro	84,378.00	3.87
Other claims on euro area credit institutions in euro	62,134.00	2.85	Liabilities to euro area residents in foreign currency	1539.00	0.07
Securities of euro area residents in euro	603,358.00	27.65	Liabilities to non-euro area residents in foreign currency	7328.00	0.34

(continued)

Sheet 4.1 (continued)

Consolidated Financial Statement of the Eurosystem (EUR Millions, January 2015)					
Assets	Amount	%	Liabilities	Amount	%
Securities held for monetary policy purposes	227,107.00	10.41	Counterpart of special drawing rights allocated by the IMF	56,374.00	2.58
Other securities	376,251.00	17.24	Other liabilities	220,434.00	10.10
General government debt in euro	26,715.00	1.22	Revaluation accounts	330,898.00	15.17
Other assets	238,362.00	10.92	Capital and reserves	95,245.00	4.37
Total assets	2,181,954.00	100.00	Total liabilities	2,181,954.00	100.00

(15.76 %), Claims on non-euro Area Residents in Foreign Currency (12.54 %). It seems more balanced assets distribution among main items in the Eurosystem. While on the Liability side, Banknotes in Circulation, which is equal to Currency in Circulation accounts the most (46.02 %). Current Accounts, which covering the minimum reserve system takes only a little more than 10 % of total.

If we re-classify all the items into different factors that providing reserve fund and different channels that sterilizing the reserve fund, we could get a Simplified Balance of Sheet in the Eurosystem (see Sheet 4.2). On the Assets side there are "Foreign," "Treasury," "Banks" and "Other" channels that provide base money in the Eurosystem. On the Liabilities side, besides "Currency Banknotes in Circulation" and "Current Accounts (minimum and excess reserve)" that constitute the "Reserve Money", there are "Bank Factors," "Foreign Factors," "Treasury Factors" and other liabilities and capital that are responsible for absorbing the reserve funds.

In this simplified balance sheet of monetary authority in the Eurosystem., we group "Securities of Euro Area Residents in Euro" and "General Government Debt in Euro" as "Base Money Treasury"; group "Gold and Gold Receivables," "Claims on Non-euro Area Resident in Foreign Currency", "Claims on Euro Area Resident in Foreign Currency" and "Claims on Non-euro Area Residents in Euro" as "Base Money Foreign"; name "Lending to Euro Area Credit Institutions in Euro" and "Other Claims on Euro Area Credit Institutions in Euro" as "Base Money Bank"; and the rest items as "Other Assets". Similarly, on the side of Liabilities, "Other Liabilities to Euro Area Credit Institutions in Euro", "Debt Certificates Issued" and "Liabilities to Other Euro Area Residents in Euro" could be grouped as "Treasury Factors"; "Counterpart of Special Drawing Rights Allocated by the IMF", "Liabilities to Non-euro Area Residents in Euro", "Liabilities to Non-euro Area Residents in Foreign Currency" and "Liabilities to Euro area Residents in Foreign Currency" as "Foreign Factors"; "Deposit facility", "Fixed-term deposits", "Fine-tuning reverse operations" and "Deposits related to margin calls" in "Liabilities to Euro Area Credit Institutions in Euro" could be described as "Bank Factors"; there are also "Revaluation Accounts" and "Other Liabilities and Capitals".

Sheet 4.2 Simplified balance of sheet

Simplified Consolidated Financial Statement of the Eurosystem (EUR Millions, January 2015)					
Assets	Amount	%	Liabilities	Amount	%
Monetary base foreign	671,739.00	30.79	Banknotes in circulation	1,004,230.00	46.02
Monetary base bank	641,780.00	29.41	Current accounts (minimum and excess reserve)	227,385.00	10.42
Monetary base treasury	630,073.00	28.88	Bank factors	37,138.00	1.70
Other assets	238,362.00	10.92	Treasury factors	117,004.00	5.36
			Foreign factors	149,619.00	6.86
			Other liabilities	220,434.00	10.10
			Revaluation accounts	330,898.00	15.17
			Capital and reserves	95,245.00	4.37
Total assets	2,181,954.00	100.00	Total liabilities	2,181,954.00	100.00

From this simplified edition, it is clear that the three major source of Base Money in the Eurosystem are almost even, respectively being about 30 %.

Meanwhile, Banknotes in Circulation constitutes almost half of the Liabilities (46.02 %). Then, Current Accounts, which covers the minimum reserve system accounts for 10.42 %. Others, say Treasury Factors, Foreign Factors as well as Bank Factors are relatively marginal in the process of sterilization.

If we define the Assets as Liquidity Supply and Liabilities as Liquidity Needs, then we can rewrite the Balance Sheet of Monetary Authority in Eurozone (see Sheet 4.3).

Two Items from Assets side, Open market operations and Marginal lending facility, "supply" the "needs" from Liabilities side, Current accounts, Deposit facility and Net liquidity effect from Autonomous factors and SMP.

Graph 4.2 provides compositions of each items more clearly.

Liquidity needs of the banking system mainly result from the minimum reserve requirements imposed on euro area credit institutions and from autonomous factors, which are not under the direct control of the ECB's liquidity management, but have an influence on the aggregate current account holdings of the banking sector.

Such factors belong to "autonomous" can be banknotes in circulation and government deposits with some national central banks. Since 1999, government deposits, aggregated at the euro area level, have continuously been the most volatile autonomous factor, causing a large part of the errors in the forecast of liquidity needs underlying the allotment decisions for the open market operations of the ECB.

As illustrated in Graph 4.2, the ECB normally aims to satisfy the liquidity needs of the banking system via its open market operations. Also, counterparties can access the Eurosystem's standing facilities with an overnight maturity.

Money Supply in the Eurosystem

Sheet 4.4 outlines the key indicators of money aggregates in the Eurosystem from 2006 to 2014. From these data, we could observe the features of monetary supply in the Eurosystem.

In the Eurosystem,

- Monetary Base = Currency in Circulation + Reserve Requirement = Currency in Circulation + (Required Reserves + Excess Reserves);
- Money Supply = (Money Multiplier) * (Monetary Base);
- *If,*

M0 = Currency in Circulation, MS = Money Supply = M3,[4] *m = Money Multiplier, B = Base Money*

$MS = m * B \rightarrow M3 = m * B \rightarrow m = M3/B$[5]

[4]We use the data of M3 as all forms of deposits in financial system.

[5]We get Currency in Circulation (M0), M3 and Base Money (Monetary Base) from the official reports.

Sheet 4.3 Further studies on the balance of sheet in the Eurosystem

Assets (liquidity supply)	Liabilities (liquidity needs)
Open market operations	Current accounts
Marginal lending facility	Deposit facility
	Net liquidity effect from autonomous factors and SMP

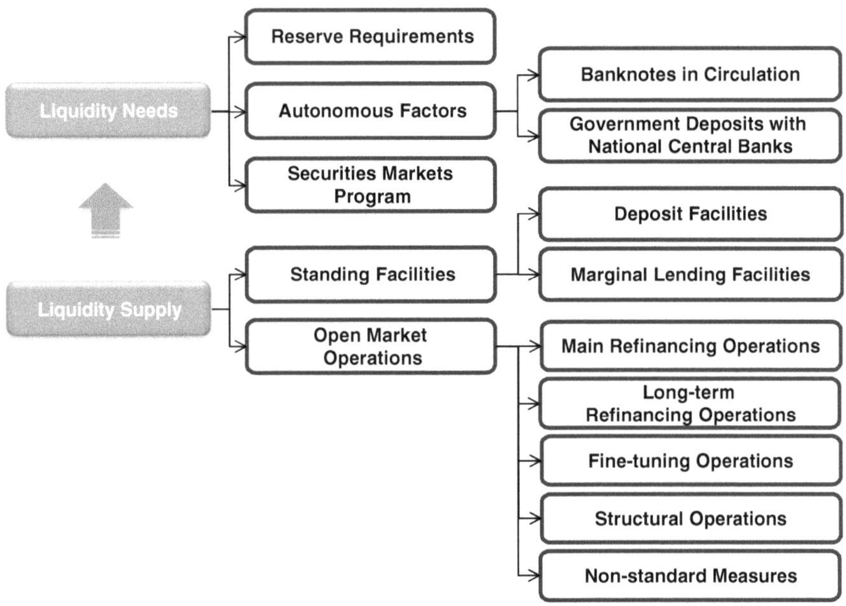

Graph 4.2 Further understanding of the balance of sheet in the Eurosystem

Also in Sheet 4.4, we can calculate the Money Multiplier in the U.S. from 2006 to 2014 directly using M3/Base Money.[6] Changes of both Currency in Circulation and Reserves seem peaceful, so does the Money Multiplier in recent years.

Money Multiplier in Eurosystem has been continuously high in some certain period. Similarly with the situation in the U.S., when the economy encountered tough time, the multiplier also declined. During the European Crisis, the multiplier was accordingly down to around 6, representing the decelerated monetary circulation.

And here are the graphs from which we can directly observe the changes of monetary base and money multipliers in the Eurosystem in the recent years (see Graphs 4.3 and 4.4).

---

[6]Money Multiplier announced by the official reports is almost the same as the Money Multiplier that calculated directly using M3/Base Money, except some certain quarters.

Sheet 4.4 Money supply and money multiplier in the Eurosystem

Eurozone in billion euro	2006 Q1	2006 Q2	2006 Q3	2006 Q4	2007 Q1	2007 Q2	2007 Q3	2007 Q4	2008 Q1	2008 Q2	2008 Q3	2008 Q4
M0 = currency in circulation	536	550	565	580	592	601	612	626	637	649	660	710
M3 = money supply	7223	7381	7566	7757	8010	8200	8411	8655	8875	9044	9218	9404
Monetary base	709	735	755	772	787	812	832	842	859	880	900	1151
Money multiplier	10.18	10.04	10.02	10.05	10.17	10.10	10.11	10.28	10.34	10.28	10.25	8.17
Eurozone in billion euro	2009 Q1	2009 Q2	2009 Q3	2009 Q4	2010 Q1	2010 Q2	2010 Q3	2010 Q4	2011 Q1	2011 Q2	2011 Q3	2011 Q4
M0 = currency in circulation	726	732	744	757	776	783	789	795	805	816	832	844
M3 = money supply	9409	9426	9402	9353	9332	9238	9265	9292	9345	9387	9481	9498
Monetary base	1056	1000	1123	1052	1183	1308	1115	1073	1061	1064	1185	1335
Money multiplier	8.91	9.43	8.37	8.89	7.89	7.07	8.31	8.66	8.81	8.82	8.00	7.11
Eurozone in billion euro	2012 Q1	2012 Q2	2012 Q3	2012 Q4	2013 Q1	2013 Q2	2013 Q3	2013 Q4	2014 Q1	2014 Q2	2014 Q3	2014 Q4
M0 = currency in circulation	852	863	867	863	868	882	894	909	925	932	948	967
M3 = money supply	9604	9652	9698	9781	9807	9823	9847	9830	9886	9964	10,088	10,306
Monetary base	1599	1762	1766	1631	1429	1295	1274	1194	1163	1172	1207	1193
Money multiplier	6.01	5.48	5.49	6.00	6.86	7.59	7.73	8.23	8.50	8.50	8.36	8.64

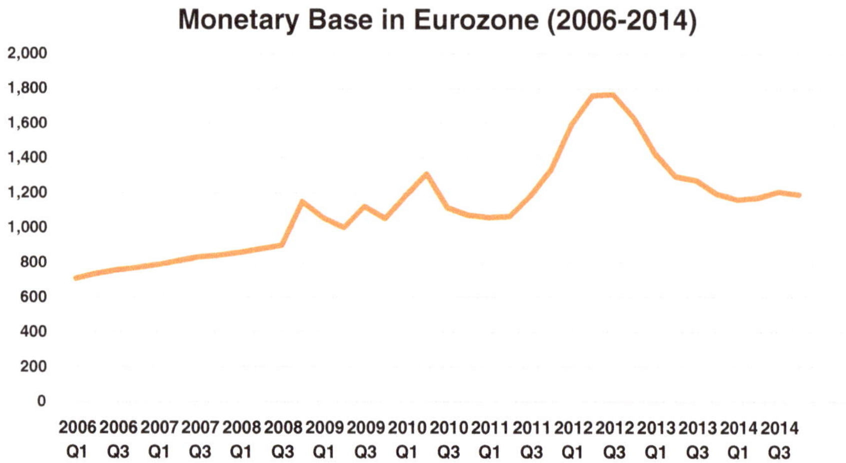

Graph 4.3 Changes of monetary base in the Eurosystem (2006–2014)

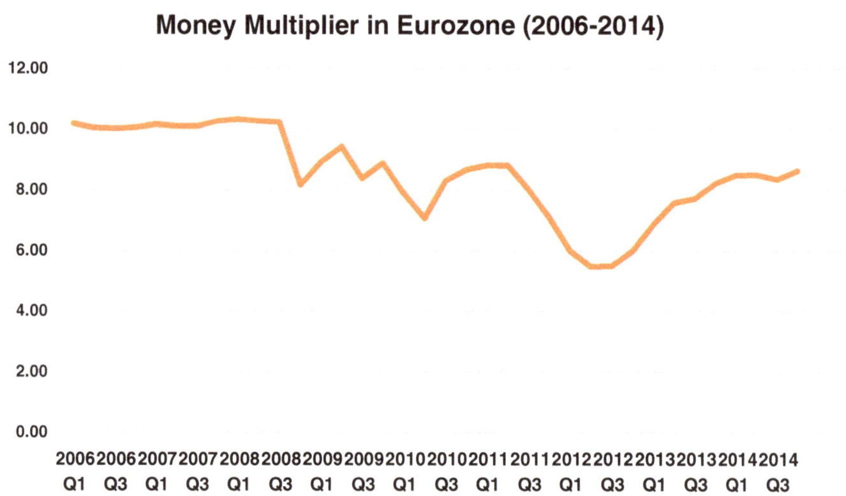

Graph 4.4 Changes of money multiplier in the Eurosystem (2006–2014)

4.2 "Creative, Ambitious, but Trapped"

Widely opposing views were expressed by economists and politicians on both sides of the Atlantic until the last minute of 1998 on the likelihood that the euro would be created and on the probability of its success if, indeed, it were established. Especially in the U.S., the Nobel Laureates Paul Samuelson, Milton Friedman, James Tobin and Robert Solow, as well as such well-known economists as Paul

Krugman and Martin Feldstein even doubted that the euro would come into existence. Of course, when it became clear that the euro would indeed be created, most skeptics predicted that it would finally fail because the European Monetary Union (EMU) was not an optimum currency area so that "a single-fit-all, EMU-wide monetary policy would lead to serious problems for the member states".

The euro and its backed system, is undoubtedly a creation, comparing with other currencies that spontaneously issued and endorsed by sovereignty. As the facts tell, a large number of prestigious economists had undervalued the creativity and will behind the regional currency.

From its very beginning, the euro has been an important international currency and is bound to become even more so in the future. The reasons are that the EMU: (a) is almost as large an economic and trading entity as the U.S., (b) has a large, well-developed and growing financial market, which is increasingly free of controls, and (c) expected to have a good inflation performance that will keep the value of the euro stable. If the international use of the euro were to match its share of would GDP, exports, and financial sector, the euro would become almost as important as the dollar as an international or vehicle currency.

It is unlikely, however, that the international use of the euro will soon match the EMU share of world GDP and exports. Obviously, as Dominick Salvatore pointed out, one reason is that the absence of a federal government drags the market for government securities in the process of integration, which is inevitably fall short of that in the U.S. Another reason is according to strict portfolio diversification motives, there is less of a reason for EMU investors to increase their holdings of euro-dominated assets, and while there will be a greater reason for them to increasing their dollar-dominated assets. They were, at least, proved in the European Debt Crisis that ten years after the euro's full circulation.

Following the U.S. financial crisis in 2008, fears of a sovereign debt crisis developed in 2009 among fiscally conservative investors concerning some European states, with the situation becoming particularly tense in early 2010. This included Eurozone members Greece, Ireland and Portugal and also some EU countries outside the area. Iceland, the country which experienced the largest crisis in 2008 when its entire international banking system collapsed, has emerged less affected by the sovereign-debt crisis as the government was unable to bail the banks out. In the EU, especially in countries where sovereign debts have increased sharply due to bank bailouts, a crisis of confidence has emerged with the widening of bond yield spreads and risk insurance on credit default swaps between these countries and other EU members, most importantly Germany. It is said that the Eurosystem was never as close to 'doomsday' as in the summer of 2012. The debt spreads of the Eurozone periphery countries surged and the epicentre of the crisis shifted from Greece and Portugal to larger economies such as Spain and Italy. To be included in the Eurozone, the countries had to fulfil certain convergence criteria, but the meaningfulness of such criteria was diminished by the fact they have not been applied to different countries with the same strictness.

On 26 July 2012, the ECB President Mario Draghi eventually announced that the Bank would do "whatever it takes (within [its] mandate)" to save the euro.

Shortly after, on 2 August 2012 the ECB declared its intention to perform outright government bond purchases. On 6 September 2012 the Bank finally formalized its lender of last resort (LOLR) role via the Outright Money Transaction (OMT) programme albeit only for those Eurozone countries who would be eligible for European Stability Mechanism funding; that is, only for solvent but illiquid countries (Wolff 2014). With hindsight, it is now clear that the OMT has been one of the most effective programmes in the recent history of central banking, bringing down the credit spreads across the Eurozone without spending a single euro under its name. This view could be strengthened by the evidence from the study of money supply in the Eurosystem above. The monetary base was soon back to stable right after the shortly adjustment during the Crisis, without permanent explosion of the balance sheet as well as soaring money supply.

However, according to the Economist Intelligence Unit in 2011, "if the [euro area] is treated as a single entity, its [economic and fiscal] position looks no worse and in some respects, rather better than that of the US or the UK" and the budget deficit for the euro area as a whole is much lower and the euro area's government debt/GDP ratio of 86 % in 2010 was about the same level as that of the United States. "Moreover", they write, "private-sector indebtedness across the euro area as a whole is markedly lower than in the highly leveraged Anglo-Saxon economies". The authors conclude that the crisis "is as much political as economic" and the result of the fact that the euro area lacks the support of "institutional paraphernalia (and mutual bonds of solidarity) of a state".

Without any question, the euro has turned into a trap for the European states that adopted it. The southern states are trapped because the inflationary credit bubble brought about by the euro deprived them of their competitiveness. The immediate reason is interest spread[7] is disappeared, however the southern Eurozone countries did not repay their debts with those saved interest payments, but to finance their public spending. This resulted an inflationary credit bubble till its bursting in 2007. While the deep reason for that is caused by the lack of fiscal discipline.

Before it was clear that the euro would come, private and public debtors in the southern European countries, as well as in Ireland, had to offer very high yields to their foreign creditors to compensate for potential exchange rate depreciations, most of the debtors' currencies having depreciated repeatedly during the previous decades. That was the main reason why the southern countries wanted the euro so badly. The new currency, they thought, would bring about a lasting reduction in exchange-risk-motivated spreads, bringing significant relief to the debtor parties.

Everything appeared to work just fine initially. Exchange rate uncertainty disappeared and interest rates converged within just two years of the Madrid Summit

[7]Interest spreads always result from the fear of investors that they might lose their money. Investors charge a premium above the interest rate that would be demanded for a presumably safe investment to compensate for the risk that the debt may not be fully repaid. It ensures that interest rate differentials (i.e. spreads) reflect the investors' risk assessment. Interest rate differentials that reflect investment risks are necessary for the 'law of one price', one of the fundamental efficiency requirements of a market economy, to hold.

of December 1995, which set the timetable for the introduction of the euro, and it became clear which countries would participate. Convergence was completed by May 1998, when the exchange rates of the 11 participating countries in the first round were irrevocably fixed. The formal introduction of the euro as legal tender between banks due to start on 1 January 1999, and the capital markets had already priced in these developments. After that point in May 1998, the interest spreads were so low that they can hardly be made out in the chart. Typically, countries like Italy or Spain had to offer an interest premium of only 20 basis points, i.e. 0.2 %, above the German bench-mark to convince investors to buy their government bonds.

The phase of nearly identical interest rates ended in summer 2007, about a decade after the convergence began and five years after the physical introduction of the euro, when the US subprime crisis spilled over to Europe and led to the collapse of the interbank market.

However, the falling interest rates did not just represent a direct cost advantage for the debtors. They also changed their behaviour, inducing them to relax their efforts at saving and to take on more debt instead.

In the Stability and Growth Pact, the member countries committed to setting up medium-term goals for righting their public finances and promised that their structural budget deficit would not exceed 1 % of GDP. A level of up to 3 % for the actual deficit was permitted in the exceptional case of an economic slump, and more than 3 % was allowed to stimulate the economy only if a country found itself in a recession in which its real GDP dropped by at least 2 % within a year. The member countries committed to adopting corrective budgetary measures if there were signs of deviation from the budget goals, as well as a prompt elimination of budget deficits. If the 3 % budget deficit limit was exceeded, the rules stipulated the levying of sanctions

But as in the case of the Maastricht Treaty itself, the rules were not obeyed, not even those that in 2005 had been watered down by limiting the possibility of imposing sanctions, after Germany and France violated them. By 2013, the 3 % deficit ceiling had been breached on 148 occasions. Among these cases, only in 51 of the 148 cases exceeding the 3 % limit would have been allowed on account of a deep-enough recession. In other words, sanctions should have been levied in 97 cases. On average, the debt-to-GDP ratio of the euro countries rose by more than 20 percentage points, from 72 to 96 %. In this light, the Eurozone itself shouldn't have been allowed into the currency union.

As Berry Eichengreen pointed years before, the real problem in the Eurosystem would be "monetary success, fiscal failure". All the creative and ambitious design would doom to be trapped only if the day comes when the Eurozone is complemented with a fiscal authority with possibly centralised tax and redistributive powers so that it eventually evolves towards a currency with a single political and fiscal union.

Chapter 5
Rising CNY: "The Elephant in the Room"

5.1 Monetary System in China

This part tries to introduce the structure of its monetary system, including its monetary authority, the decision-making process and the main instruments of its monetary policy, and thereby understands the money supply in China.

5.1.1 Structure of the Monetary Authority in China

In China, the State Council represents the central government to hold the power of economic management. However, the final decisive body is an even higher-level special group, known as the Central Financial and Economic Leading Group of Communist Party of China. This Group, composed of all top governors from relevant fields as well as the Premier and directly led by the Politburo of the CPC Central Committee, is responsible for conducting the policies and making the decisions on the State monetary affairs.

According to the Law of People's Republic of China on the People's Bank of China, the central bank in China is the People's Bank of China (PBC), which is thereby the main body to propose and to implement the monetary policy. It needs to report to the State Council its decisions concerning the annual money supply, interest rates, exchange rates and other important issues specified by the State Council for approval before they are put into effect. It is also obliged to submit work reports to the Standing Committee of the National People's Congress on the implementation of monetary policy and the performance of the financial industry. In the central bank, different divisions held their own special responsibilities, among which Currency Gold and Silver Bureau is in charge of the State gold reserves and State Treasury Bureau manages the State treasury as fiscal agent, etc. State

J. Wang, *The Past and Future of International Monetary System*,
SpringerBriefs in Economics, DOI 10.1007/978-981-10-0164-2_5

Administration of Foreign Exchange is affiliated to the PBC and is responsible for international payments and foreign exchange markets.

There is also a key consultative body in the PBC called Monetary Policy Committee, whose responsibility is to advise on the formulation and the adjustment of monetary policy and policy targets for a certain period, the application of monetary policy instrument, the major monetary policy measures and the coordination between monetary policy and other macroeconomic policies. This Committee is composed of high-level representatives from State Council, PBC, State Development and Reform Commission, Minister of Finance, State Administration of Foreign Exchange, China Banking Regulatory Commission, China Securities Regulatory Commission, China Insurance Regulatory Commission, National Bureau of Statistics, China Association of Banks and an expert from the academia. In such a high-level and comprehensive collaborated network, opinions expressed and approved by the Committee meetings should be filed as an annex to the proposed decisions of the PBC that to be reported to the State Council for approval.

Besides those core monetary entities, there still are a number of economic administrations that should not be ignored in understanding China's monetary system. Minister of Finance, above all, is parallel to People's Bank of China and is in charge of issuing Treasury Bonds and negotiating foreign liabilities. Three Regulatory Commissions—China Banking Regulatory Commission, China Securities Regulatory Commission and China Insurance Regulatory Commission collectively play a supervisory role on China's financial markets as well as China Association of Banks (see Graph 5.1).

So far, it could be concluded that People's Bank of China, the central bank, plays the main role in the monetary system in China, but on the decisive position of the system still lies the State Council. However, the following studies could be considered as the outcomes of a unified "Monetary Authority" in China.

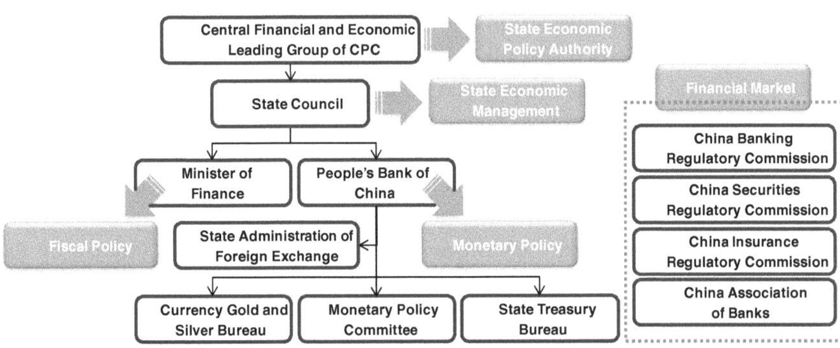

Graph 5.1 Monetary authority and related institutions in China

5.1.2 *The Central Bank in China*

Although not being as a completely independent, decisive authority in China's monetary system, the People's Bank of China still processes an important position of proposing and carrying out State monetary policies, as well as regulating domestic financial markets. Therefore, it's necessary to take a close look at the performance of this central bank on managing the money in China.

(1) *Objectives of the People's Bank of China*

To maintain the stability of the value of Chinese Yuan (CNY) and thereby promoting the economic growth are the main goals of the PBC as a central bank.

In practice, the PBC also holds the responsibilities to safeguard the State financial stability, to insure the operation of payment and settlement systems, and to develop the consolidation of financial statistics so as to conduct economic analysis and forecast.

(2) *Main Responsibilities of the People's Bank of China*

The PBC's major functions are provided by the amended Law of the People's Republic of China on the People's Bank of China, adopted by the 6th meeting of the Standing Committee of the 10th National People's Congress on December 27, 2003. According to its role as a central bank, these functions can be divided into three categories:

Enforcement of State monetary policies

The PBC is responsible for proposing and implementing monetary policy (including foreign exchange rate policy), issuing CNYas well as administering its circulation.

Supervision of State monetary system

It owns the power of regulating State financial markets (including the inter-bank lending markets, the inter-bank bond markets, foreign exchange markets and gold markets).

Management of State treasury

It also holdsofficial reservesand managesState treasury as a fiscal agent.

(3) *Main Instruments of the Monetary Policy in China*

- Compulsory Reserve Requirement
- Central Bank Base Interest Rate
- Re-loan and Re-discount Rate
- Open Market Operation

(4) *Balance Sheet of Monetary Authority of China*

In order to be better illustrated and compared, it is necessary to clarify some of the items from the official balance sheet of People' Bank of China, especially to those whose definitions are full of Chinese characteristics.

First of all, in China's financial system, all financial institutions can be divided into three main categories according to their different basic functions in the financial system: Monetary Authority, Deposit Money Banks and Non-monetary Financial Institutions. Monetary Authority manages and supervises the whole system with the responsibility of creating and injecting base money into the system. Deposit Money Banks (e.g., Commercial Banks) play the role of absorbing deposits and making the money multiplier into effect thereby creating deposits. Comparatively, Non-monetary Financial Institutions are such a group of financial institutions that cannot create any deposits in circulation. It includes Special Depository Institutions (e.g., Trust Investment, Financial Lease, Housing Loan, Foreign Banks and other Financial Companies) and Other Financial Corporations (e.g., Insurance Company, Security Company and Pension Fund): the former one still have the ability of absorbing deposits while another one are not. Therefore, it can be concluded that in China, Financial Institutions can also be divided into Depository Corporations and Non-depository Financial Institutions according to their different nature of capital sources. Both Deposit Money Banks and Special Depository Institutions are called Other Depository Corporations; they are belonging to Depository Corporations along with Monetary Authority (see Graph 5.2). Moreover, all the Other Depository Corporations are subject to Reserve Requirement.

From the official balance of sheet of monetary authority in China, we have several items to be explained (see Sheet 5.1).

Claims on Government in China only refer to those claims with the central government.

Claims on Other Depository Corporations represent the Re-loan and Re-discount to commercial banks from central bank. It used to be the main monetary policy tool but gradually faded during the past decades.

Claims on Other Financial Corporations here mainly consist of the credits to four special Assets Management Corporations established in 2004 that in order to deal with the huge bad accounts from the major commercial banks during their reformation process.

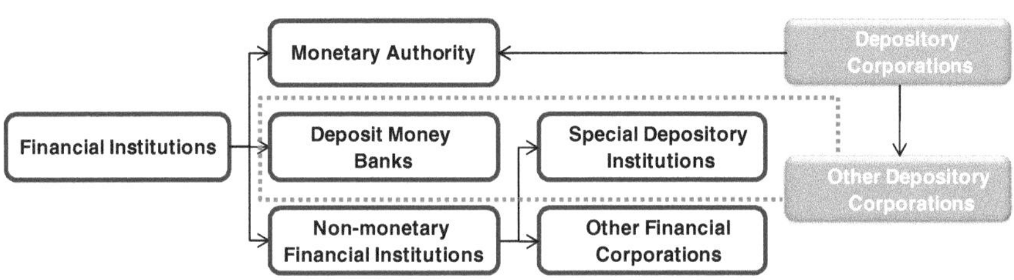

Graph 5.2 Financial institutions in China

Sheet 5.1 Official balance of sheet from monetary authority in China

Balance sheet of monetary authority in China January, 2015 Unit: 100 Million Yuan		Percentage (%)
Foreign assets	278,606.09	82.22
Foreign exchange	270,688.81	79.88
Monetary gold	669.84	0.20
Other foreign assets	7247.4382	2.14
Claims on central government	15,312.73	4.52
Claims on other depository corporations	25,789.62	7.61
Claims on other financial corporations	7848.81	2.32
Claims on non-financial sector	11.66	0.00
Other assets	11,299.13	3.33
Total assets	338,868.05	100.00
Reserve money	288,343.85	85.09
Currency issue	69,461.11	20.50
Deposits of other depository corporations	218,882.75	64.59
Deposits of financial corporations excluded from reserve money	1505.38	0.44
Bond issue	6522.00	1.92
Foreign liabilities	1561.64	0.46
Deposits of government	37,803.05	11.16
Own capital	219.75	0.06
Other liabilities	2912.37	0.86
Total liabilities	338,868.05	100.00

The item of Currency Issue includes all Currency in Circulation (the currency held by households, enterprises, cash in vault by banks and foreign holders).

Deposits of Other Depository Corporations represent all their reserve money of the central bank (Compulsory Reserve) and those with the central bank (Excess Reserve).

Bond Issue in China is a unique tool of liquidity sterilization. It refers to a special kind of bond called the Central Bank Bondwith different maturity from 3 months to three years that issued by the PBC through Open Market Operation.

Foreign Liabilities include the loan from the World Bank, Asian Development Bank or other foreign governments.

Sheet 5.1 gives us a first glance at the current feature (on January, 2015) of money stock in China. According to the data, Foreign Assets accounts for over 82 % of the total Assets, of which almost all come from Foreign Exchange. On the other side, total reserves from commercial banks that either with or of the central bank are at record level. It seems to be in accordance with the fact that in the recent years the compulsory reserve rate has been used as the main tool of the liquidity sterilization. Besides, Deposits of Government as another important tool of the central bank liquidity management attributes more than 10 % of the sterilization.

Sheet 5.2 Simplified balance of sheet

Simplified balance sheet of monetary authority in China (Unit: 100 Million Yuan January, 2015)					
Base money foreign	278,606.09	82.22 %	Currency issue (currency in circulation)	69,461.11	20.50 %
Base money treasury	15,312.73	4.52 %	Reserve requirement (compulsory and excess)	218,882.75	64.59 %
Base money banks	33,650.10	9.93 %	Bank factors	8027.38	2.37 %
Other assets	11,299.13	3.33 %	Foreign factors	1561.64	0.46 %
			Treasury factors	37,803.05	11.16 %
			Other liabilities	2912.37	0.86 %
			Own capital	219.75	0.06 %
Total assets	338,868.05	100.00 %	Total liabilities	338,868.05	100.00 %

If we rethink and try to classify all the items from the balance of sheet, we get another simplified one by which a clearer overview of China's money stock could be obtained (see Sheet 5.2).

This time, it is very clear that the foreign channel, which represents the base money created from the net surplus of foreign trades and all claims on other foreign economic entities, is the largest source of China's Base Money. Followed is the inter-banks channel in which the central bank plays its function as the "last lender", issues the central bank bond or operates re-loan and re-discount courses with the commercial banks and other financial intermediaries. Base money created by the government through issuing Treasury bond accounts for about 4.5 %.

On the other hand, after the sterilization of three different factors, "Bank Factor", "Treasury Factor" as well as "Foreign Factor", and other liabilities, Currency issue and Reserve Requirement together represent total amount of base money that create by the central bank. It is noted that in order to avoid excessive liquidity in the economy, reserve requirementshave been accumulated to such a large amount that even showed some evidence of oversized.

5.1.3 Money Supply in China

(1) *Main Patterns of Money Supply*

After learning the sources and absorbing factors of base money, we could have a look at the transmission mechanism from monetary policy into money supply in China. The monetary authority masters the courses of creating money supply and injecting them into circulation through the following four main patterns.

Treasury Path

It is no long allowed by the law for the Treasury to overdraft money directly from the central bank. The amount of money is created (lent) to the Treasury (central government) by the central bank through buying the Treasury Bonds issued by the Government. The amount of money then injected by the Treasury into production, circulation and consumption through public expenditure, transfer payment and other fiscal policy, finally becomes currency income of enterprises and individuals. Consequently, this amount of income comes back as the increased reserves requirements from all other depository corporations with or of the central bank.

Bank Path

The central bank re-loans as the "last lender" or re-finances the commercial banks through re-discount operation in order to provide the base money. The amount of base money then enlarged by the money multiplier to meet the demand of liquidity of the economy. It is historically the main pattern of creating the base money.

Foreign Path

The central bank creates the base money through purchasing foreign exchange from commercial banks. At the moment, it is the main but struggling pattern in China forced by the huge number of foreign exchange overflew continuously in the recent years. In order to keep the current pegging foreign exchange rate policy, the central bank in China has to recycle the excessive foreign exchange by creating the matching amount of CNY currency into circulation, pulling the economy into an embarrassment situation.

Central Bank Bond Path

From 2003, the PBC began to issue its own Central Bank Bond to help adjust the amount of base money. Meanwhile, this kind of bond was also considered as a supplement to the shortage of the Treasury bond in the open market operation.

The central bank withdraws the liquidity by selling the bonds to commercial banks or financial institutions in the open market. On the opposite, the amount of money is created by the central bank through repurchasing the bonds.

Example: A Closer Look at the Balance of Sheet of PBoC (the Establishment of CIC in 2007)

In August

Treasury issued Bonds to acquire money → Treasury got the Money and Commercial Banks got the Bonds:
Liabilities: Deposits of Government +
Reserve Money (Financial Corporations) −
Treasury used the Money to buy Foreign Exchange from the Central Bank → Treasury got the Foreign Exchanges and the PBC got the Money:
Assets: Foreign Assets (Foreign Exchange) −
Liabilities: Deposits of Government −

Central Bank purchased the Treasury Bonds from the Commercial Banks → Central Bank got the Claims and Commercial Banks got the Money:
Assets: Claims on Government +
Liabilities: Reserve Money (Financial Corporations) +
So far, Treasury got enough Foreign Exchanges to be the Capital of CIC.

In September
Treasury issued Bonds to acquire money → Treasury got the Money and Commercial Banks got the Bonds:
Liabilities: Deposits of Government +
Reserve Money (Financial Corporations) −
Treasury used the Money to buy the shareholders of Central Huijin Investment Ltd. from the Central Bank → Treasury got the assets and PBC got the money:
Assets: Other Assets −
Liabilities: Deposits of Government −
Finally, Treasury succeeded to turn the Foreign Exchanges into the Capital of Chinese first Sovereign Fund, CIC.

(2) *Base Money and Money Multiplier*

Sheet 5.3 outlines the key indicators of money aggregates in China from 2006 to 2014. From these data, we could observe the features of monetary supply in China.

In China,

- Monetary Base = Currency in Circulation + Reserve Requirement = Currency in Circulation + (Required Reserves + Excess Reserves);
- Money Supply = (Money Multiplier) * (Monetary Base);
- *If,*
  M0 = Currency in Circulation, MS = Money Supply = M2,[1] *m = Money Multiplier, B = Base Money*
  $MS = m * B \rightarrow M2 = m * B \rightarrow m = M2/B$[2]

[1]We use the data of M2 as all forms of deposits in financial system.

[2]We get Currency in Circulation (M0), M2 and Base Money (Monetary Base) from the official reports.

Sheet 5.3 Money supply and money multiplier in China

China in billion yuan	2006 Q1	2006 Q2	2006 Q3	2006 Q4	2007 Q1	2007 Q2	2007 Q3	2007 Q4	2008 Q1	2008 Q2	2008 Q3	2008 Q4
M0 = currency in circulation	2347	2347	2569	2707	2739	2688	2903	3033	3043	3018	3172	3422
M2 = money supply	31,049	32,276	33,187	34,558	36,410	37,783	39,310	40,340	42,305	44,314	45,290	47,517
Monetary base	6230	6278	6587	7736	7657	8222	8778	10,107	10,405	11,525	11,725	12,901
Money Multiplier	4.98	5.14	5.04	4.47	4.76	4.60	4.48	3.99	4.07	3.84	3.86	3.68
China in billion yuan	*2009 Q1*	*2009 Q2*	*2009 Q3*	*2009 Q4*	*2010 Q1*	*2010 Q2*	*2010 Q3*	*2010 Q4*	*2011 Q1*	*2011 Q2*	*2011 Q3*	*2011 Q4*
M0 = currency in circulation	3375	3364	3679	3825	3908	3890	4185	4463	4485	4448	4715	5075
M2 = money supply	53,063	56,895	58,541	60,623	64,995	67,392	69,647	72,585	75,813	78,082	78,741	85,159
Monetary base	12,417	12,384	13,330	14,384	14,989	15,407	16,117	18,513	19,257	20,347	21,220	22,464
Money Multiplier	4.27	4.59	4.39	4.21	4.34	4.37	4.32	3.92	3.94	3.84	3.71	3.79
China in billion yuan	*2012 Q1*	*2012 Q2*	*2012 Q3*	*2012 Q4*	*2013 Q1*	*2013 Q2*	*2013 Q3*	*2013 Q4*	*2014 Q1*	*2014 Q2*	*2014 Q3*	*2014 Q4*
M0 = currency in circulation	4960	4928	5343	5466	5546	5406	5649	5857	5833	5695	5884	6026
M2 = money supply	89,557	92,499	94,369	97,415	103,586	105,440	107,738	110,652	116,069	120,959	120,205	122,837
Monetary base	22,668	22,805	23,603	25,235	25,365	25,778	26,314	27,102	27,474	27,990	28,530	29,409
Money Multiplier	3.95	4.06	4.00	3.86	4.08	4.09	4.09	4.08	4.22	4.32	4.21	4.18

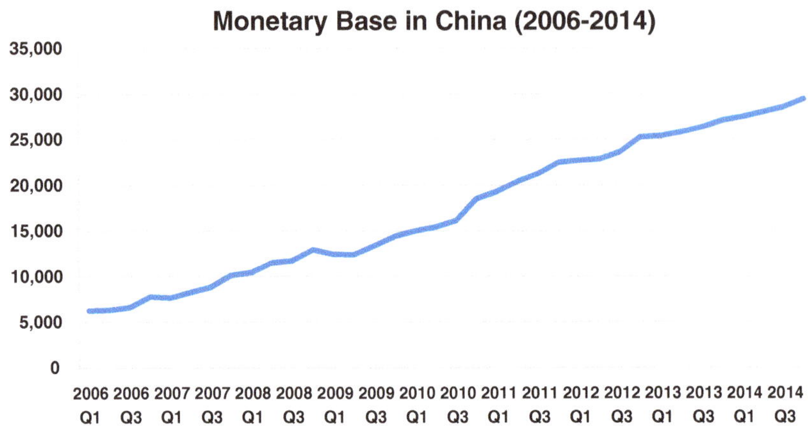

Graph 5.3 Changes of monetary base in China (2006–2014)

Graph 5.4 Changes of money multiplier in China (2006–2014)

Also in Sheet 5.3, we can calculate the Money Multiplier in China from 2006 to 2014 directly using M2/Base Money.[3] Changes ofthe Money Multiplier performance stable in recent years.

And here are the graphs from which we can directly observe the changes of monetary base and money multipliers in China in the recent years (see Graphs 5.3 and 5.4).

[3]Money Multiplier announced by the official reports is almost the same as the Money Multiplier that calculated directly using M2/Base Money, except some certain quarters.

From the quarterly data calculated above, the Money Multiplier in China in recent years floated between 3.68 and 5.14, reaching its records during the year of 2006 from which now can be considered as prelude for high speed of economic expansion in 2007. Also we can find since 2010, the Monetary Authority in China began to adjust the monetary policy to anti-inflation, resulting in the decrease of the Money Multiplier.

The trend of the monetary base in China is continuously increasing, which partly illustrates the development in China. But, still, from the components of the Money Multiplier in China, Compulsory Reserves, among other things, take the largest part.

5.2 Path Toward International Money

Compare to other countries, China's monetary system possesses its own characteristics.

The introductions above, especially this simplified Sheet 5.2 precisely tells the monetary scenario in China. It cannot be denied that under decades of the export-oriented strategy, China has successfully achieved employment promotion, external amelioration and economic development. Especially after the "Eastern-Asian Model" had crashed in the late 90s financial crisis and more recently the increasing skepticism roused among the western capitalist world, there once be a call for so-called "Beijing Consensus" which reflects the consciousness about the rise of China. However, this seemly successful case is suffering somewhat of pain in the vein of its economy, the money, at the same time.

There are two prominent problems that pushed the monetary authority in China and its policies into an embarrassing situation, passive and inefficient.

One is from the "source". From Sheet 5.2, it can be realized that the huge accumulation of foreign exchange reserves has become more and more a burden for sustainable and balanced development. Long-term of large amount of trade surplus has resulted in equally imbalanced surge of foreign exchange inwards, not to mention a continuous movement of international capitals in the same direction. Consequently, the monetary authority is faced with a challenge of the quantity of base money. Graph 5.5 provides a comparison of changes in quantity between foreign exchange reserves and base money in China from 2006 to 2011. It is quite clear that there is a high correlation between the two.

In order to manage the money supply on a sensible level so as to maintain a stable and acceptable price, the PBC has to increase the Compulsory Reserve Rate or to issue the central bank bonds in the open market. This exposes another problem in China's monetary authority, which is, the limitation of monetary instruments. Because of the decentralization of the decision-making mechanism in the monetary affairs in China, as mentioned before, the effectiveness of monetary instruments chose by the PBC would be offset or restrained by different interests from different institutions. So far, the PBC used compulsory reserve rate as its main tool to

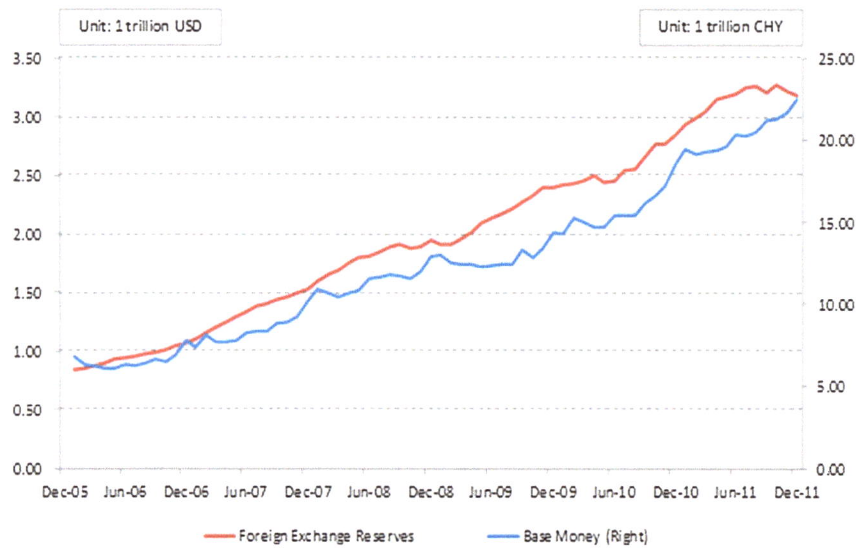

Graph 5.5 Correlations between foreign exchange reserves and base money in China (2011). *Source* website of the People's Bank of China, http://www.pbc.gov.cn

sterilize excessive money creation. However, in the beginning of 2012, this rate has reached more than 20 % while still with the pressure of future price rising. More recently, critics aroused in the country upon the unsatisfactory performance of the PBC in monetary management. Fairly speaking, it is beyond the ability of the PBC to solve this tough problem all by itself.

To jump out of the vicious circle, it should be clarified that the reasons are from two aspects which are rooted in China's economic structure. One is the external imbalance, and the other lies in the foreign exchange regime. At first glance, China possesses great domestic markets. However, most of them are under-development. Rather backward infrastructures in large areas of inland China and high propensity for saving of the residents obstruct domestic demands, which are crucial for the country to rebalance its balance of trade as well as to relief from its annoyance of huge foreign reserves. The recent large-scale of fixed investments, e.g. high-speed rail and the improvement of social security system are reflecting this kind of consideration. As for the foreign exchange regime, the monetary authority had started the process of reformation. In 2005, the first step was made, changing China's foreign exchange regime from a pure fixed exchange rate to a relatively hybrid exchange rate regime with reference to a basket of currencies, in which dollar and euro account for a larger proportion according to their important statue as China's trading partners. Graph 5.6 shows the changes of yuan against dollar during the process of the reformation on exchange rate regime. It is noticed that after the announcement of reformation, yuan underwent a slow appreciation against dollar, from 8.27 (before the reformation) to 7.8073. In the year of 2007, the trend was

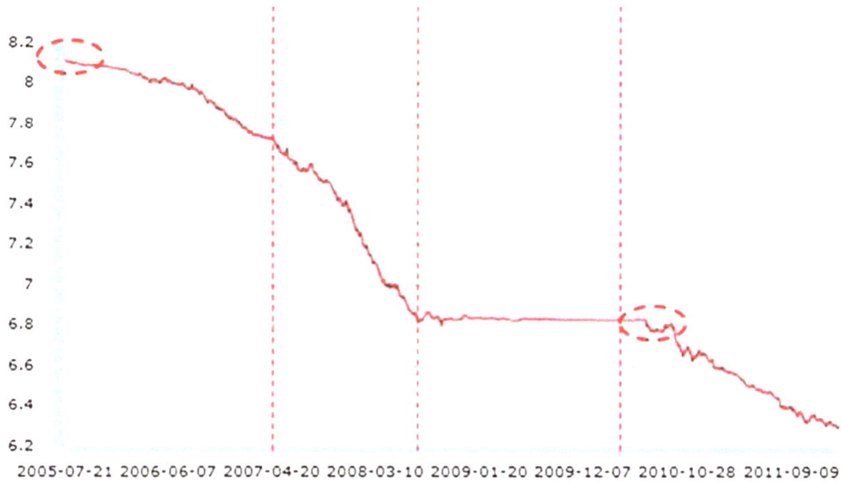

Graph 5.6 Changes of CHY/USD from 2005 to 2011. *Source* website of the People's Bank of China, http://www.pbc.gov.cn

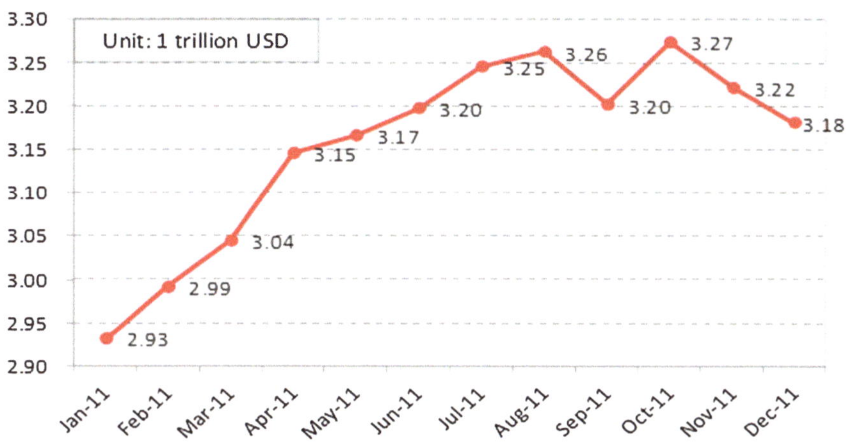

Graph 5.7 Changes of foreign exchange reserves in 2011

accelerated owing to high speed of economic growth at that time, reaching a historic exchange rate of 6.8128 in the middle of 2008. But after that, it kept almost unchanged for two years during the financial crisis until a new wave of cry pushed the reformation into second round. Then, the exchange rate continuously experienced appreciation. On February 17th, 2012, it was recorded 6.2951 against dollar. The cumulative appreciation has been more than 30 %.

One of the results would be the improvement of China's balance of trade. It was reported by General Administration of Customs that from January to September,

2011, the amount of trade surplus was $107.1 billion, decreasing 10.6 % compared to the same period of last year. Accordingly, there is a decrease of foreign exchange reserves in the late 2011 (see Graph 5.7).

It is no doubt that the reformation of exchange rate regime in China and also its monetary system still has a long way to go; otherwise, it may not only fail to be commensurate with China's international status and influence in the effort for building a new international monetary order, but also lose the opportunity to carry out its own sustainable development and fulfill bright prospect on the road to revival.

Chapter 6
Supranational SDRs: Another Way Worth Trying?

It is agreed in principle, that any national currency that issued and supervised by the national monetary authority should be a sort of sovereignty affairs. The monetary policies, along with fiscal policies, are the main instruments for national economic management in modern country. Suppose every country being ran successfully in an economy of autarchy or self-sufficiency, then the objective (s) of its monetary policies should be focus only on its domestic economic needs. Generally speaking, it could be thought as a sort of task to find the equilibrium between interest rate to promote the economic growth and inflation rate to keep the price acceptable.

However, the real world is an open economy; the process of interdependence between countries is nothing but a reality, which has further developed in the era of globalization. In addition, the monetary affairs, for their nature of high liquidity and their roles as an intermediary in economic activities, are among the top of this interdependent spectrum. These realities cause the international community to try to establish a system that facilitates the cross-border economic activities, thus promoting the world prosperity. This system, therefore, should include an international standard to be a basis of international trade and hence for the de facto monetary system; arrangements of foreign exchange rate regime that help keep stable of the currencies that interact with each other; and disciplines or agreements when adjustments for rebalance are necessary.

In modern history, the world has benefited from some well integrated international financial order. The first time would be from the 1870s to the outbreak of World War I in 1914, sometimes known as the First age of Globalization. By that time, some geographic money unions were operating effectively, including the Latin Monetary Union (France, Italy, Belgium, and Switzerland) and Scandinavian Monetary Union (Denmark, Norway and Sweden). In a Union, each currency was accepted legally by members. In the case when currency without membership, widespread participation in the gold standard would be supplemented. Great Britain's more capital exports helped to adjust the imbalances, thus compensating other states for income lost from export of goods. Despite this organically evolved and well ran system, the world wars pushed the world into a volatility period of time.

After the Second World War, the Bretton Woods System was created by a plan that endorsed by 42 countries. The system introduced a fixed but adjustable

J. Wang, *The Past and Future of International Monetary System*,
SpringerBriefs in Economics, DOI 10.1007/978-981-10-0164-2_6

exchange rate regime where the currencies were pegged against the dollar, with the dollar itself convertible into gold at a fixed price of $35 per ounce. It was so-called a gold–dollar exchange standard. Meanwhile, two international institutions, the IMF and the World Bank were created. This designed monetary system ran well for decades until the challenge predicted by Mr. Triffin and described as the "Triffin Dilemma" became pressing. The dual use of dollar as an international standard as well as a national currency pulled it into a dilemma situation: on one hand, the increasing international demand forced the US to run a trade deficit, which unavoidably eroded confidence in dollar as a standard. Meanwhile, a parallel market for gold where the soared price encouraged speculators running down the US gold reserves appeared and quickly developed. All of these pressures finally pushed the U.S. to end the convertibility into gold in 1971, which brought the end of the Bretton Woods systems.

Until now, the post Bretton Wood system is sometimes called the "Washington Consensus", or described by others a transition that "was marked by a switch from a state led to a market led system", resulting in a system of floating exchange rates. The dollar so far, remains its predominant position in the system. Due to uncontrolled capital movements, floating exchange rate and other characteristics of this system, financial sectors worldwide has gained some high rates of return; the depth and the width of globalization have achieved historic records. While on the other hand, financial and economic crises have been more intense and have increased in their frequency and damaging effects as well. There is some reason to believe that the architecture of current international monetary system has behaved well, despite some weaknesses that it exposed already.

One is the "Triffin Dilemma". To find out the solution against the "Dilemma", the IMF created a new international reserve asset, the Special Drawing Rights (SDRs), under the fixed exchange regime at that time, in order to supplement the shortage of gold and to introduce the amount of dollar that needed by the world trade. Its price was designed to be fixed to gold and by the initial time equal $1. The name of SDRs exactly described the initial designed function of its creation. How does it work? What about its historic performance and why? What happen if the international standard becomes the SDRs? Is it another way worth trying if we want to cope with the weaknesses of current system?

The other one is due to the fast growing environment. The world today is no longer what it was yesterday. It is unwise to defend the status-quo with ignorance of the new changes. As the dollar surpassed the British pound in the early 20th century, the group of international moneys witnessed the Japanese yen's inclusion. Following, came the introduction of the euro. Each time, the call for a change to the system represented the rising power and the new demand of development behind it. Nowadays, the current system has been under the challenge from the emerging economies. It is true that soon after the Asian Financial Crisis, the developing world as a whole stopped running current account deficits and experienced a consistent, fast growth. Among them, China is doubtless outstanding, followed by Brazil, India, Russia and others. The emerging economies are de facto important participants in the international monetary system. They get more and more influence in the world trade network and become more and more interdependent with the advanced countries. There is a call for re-recognition of these geopolitical changes. Otherwise, the current system would be sooner or later run out of control. Therefore, it is time to listen to the voices from the emerging world and let them participant, thus taking their responsibilities for the system-build project.

6.1 The Methods for Establishing the SDRs and Its Working System

6.1.1 The Background of Trying Another Way

It is accepted that for the nature of the real world economy, and so the needs for certain orders that proposed and agreed among economic participants, the international monetary system exists and changes. The functions of an international monetary system include widely accepted currencies to facilitate international trade and cross-border investment, as well as a corresponding foreign exchange regime. A system should also provide supporting institutions such as instruments of settlements, payments and adjustments by which the world interdependent activities could be accomplished. At the center of every workable international monetary system lies the international standard, which can be used as:

- an international liquidity that is necessary to meet the demands of international financial activities and the world economic development; and
- an international reserve assets that is to represent the reallocation of capital among countries.

By "standard" it means, this kind of monetary intermediary should possess the merits of both stable and freely useable.

Times of trials of establishing an international standard proved it to be a task that always along with controversies and imperfections. In the past, gold had surpassed other metals to be long and widely adopted as a world monetary standard especially in the era rested on the conversion of paper notes into preset quantities of gold. According to the classical definition, money has the responsibilities to be an intermediary of exchange (or a measurement of value), an instrument of savings, a tool of domestic payment and an international currency. Gold, in its nature, is born money, especially in the highly diversified international monetary environment. Gold standard ensured the stability during most of commercial economy and the early stage of capitalism; however, it was confronted with embarrassment after unprecedented economic prosperity and waves of globalizations. The nature that helps it get the acknowledgement as a perfect standard, in turn, prevents it from long being. It is true that the limit quantity of gold failed to meet the criteria of "sufficient liquidity" of an international standard. In addition to that, the geographically imbalanced distribution of gold sometimes made certain countries preferred position to others.

Therefore, another “ever-lasting” form of standard, the so-called paper money backed by the power of its issued country was introduced. First the pound sterling endorsed by the Great Britain, then followed the US dollar representing the superpower after two world wars. This new kind of standard was created in order to avoid the shortage of gold and was guaranteed by, from time to time, the strongest economic and political entity behind it. After the Second World War, despite times of “dollar shortage”, this national currency standard served the world economy for decades. However, as national interests, the US prefers politically to avoid the constraint of the convertibility to gold and economically to leave the dollar floating so as to gain the trade benefits from currency depreciation, thus promoting the domestic economic growth. These proved the dual use of dollar as a national currency as well as an international standard has an inner contradiction. Today, the cumulative huge deficits in its trade balance have pushed both the dollar and its leading system on the edge: even more risks would be created if the US goes on coping this situation with implementing rounds of Quantitative Easing (QEs) and let “dollar glut” flooded to every corner of the world to weaken the credibility of the biggest power and its backed system.

There are more and more voices calling for retrospections on the trials of international standard, especially for those who have existed already. In this background, the Special Drawing Rights (SDRs, or called paper gold), which was firstly issued by the IMF in 1970, is highlighted among others. The SDRs was initially proposed to be a possible solution against the “Triffin Dilemma” caused by a national currency that held the responsibility as an international standard. This famous and original analysis of the post war international monetary system which was, in the name of its proposer, the Belgian/US economist Robert Triffin, illustrated that the international monetary system agreed at the Bretton Woods would not run for long because its inner contradiction. That was, since the gold’s supply as an international standard was limited and uneven in a fixed gold-dollar exchange standard regime, the new trying of national currency (the US dollar, in fact) should provide sufficient international liquidity through its own payments deficits. However this sort of deficits would be bound to undermine the confidence in the paper dollar. Therefore, a dilemma of choice lied in between running short of international liquidity and undermining the confidence in the national currency. This situation was predicted to cause a crisis sooner or later and it had been proved in the past few years. Even worse, the system was lack of any binding conventions for countries to adjust their payments positively such as to revalue the foreign exchange rate.

Against the “Dilemma”, the IMF then created the SDRs in 1968. Until the year of 2009, discussion upon the issue of SDRs had reached its climax with the governor of the People’s Bank of China, Zhou Xiaochuan, implicitly proposing that the SDRs should gradually displace the dollar at the center of the international monetary system so that surplus countries like China should be able to convert their official dollar holdings into SDRs or SDRs-denominated assets.

6.1.2 *The Methodology of Establishing the SDRs and Its Working System*

To better understanding the principles and the methodology of establishing the SDRs, it is necessary to compare it with the dollar standard system.

(1) *Establishment Methods*

The SDRs-centered system has the different establishing methods with the dollar-centered system, or precisely called the national currency-centered system.

First, the reserve supply mechanism. For a dollar-centered system, or any other national currency instead, it provides the international reserves through the national balance sheets. In other words, the supply is in fact to be a response to the exogenous demand from outside. If the world economy expands, then so does simultaneously the supply of the reserve money. It is quite clear that the amount of international reserves can be by no means affordable by a single national economy, even if it has used to be such a super power. In practice, this centered country, has to run a payments deficit to meet the needs of its currency just like the US does today. On the other hand, however, the supply of SDRs is decided by an administrative agreement within the IMF rather than following the world economic needs. And the increase of the SDRs would not require any necessary deficits on national balance of payments which could in turn erode the confidence of the system someday.

Second, one of the important reasons to establish a supranational currency as the international reserves like SDRs is to avoid some national privilege in the process of monetary issuing. There are at least two aspects of the so-called "privilege": One is seigniorage which refers to the gains from the issuer by issuing the very low-interest asset of money (the paper dollar) as an international reserve asset while making a high-interest loan to the reserve-holding countries. The other one is that the national issuer, the US for instance has the privilege to pay also its foreign debts in its own money, or by its unlimited increase of liabilities rather than an "assets transfer". To avoid an international standard to be indulged in narrow national interests, the SDRs was designed to be the world's reserve base and was controlled by the IMF. In a SDRs centered system, the amount of SDRs supply is followed by a long-run monetary growth and is decided by an agreement in the IMF. The supranational standard, along with the fixed supply of gold is then created as a base or primary international reserve. Countries with an initial allocation of SDRs, can decide to hold other foreign exchange reserves such as dollar that firmly pegged with SDRs or make their reserve holdings as a source of domestic money supply. Therefore, by transferring the international base reserve from a national currency to SDRs, it is the IMF, a supranational institution who is in charge with the monetary evolution of the world.

Third, there is an issue about adjustment. It is essential for an international monetary system to set up some "disciplines" of adjustment when world imbalance occurs. Under the current dollar-centered system, as we already know, the increases in international reserve come from an increase in the external deficits of the United States. They are financed by the surplus of the rest of the world. It has some reason to believe that this kind of imbalance will go further untila predictable but unacceptable collapse finally breaks out. Before that, there is lack of agreement for adjustment than purely national considerations. The SDRs though, are designed to be a mechanism in which the pressure of adjustment would not be focused on the bilateral relations. It is a potential claim on the freely usable currencies of IMF members. The motivation of revaluation of its currency lies on the country's own external imbalance but not on the demand of its counterpart. That will help to avoid the embarrassment like China encounters today.

(2) *Decision Process*

In the SDRs working system, the IMF is designed to be at the center. It is the international organization who makes the decision on the amount of the SDRs allocation, its valuation method, its interest rate benchmarks and also, plays as a broker in the process of international adjustment. Therefore, it is necessary to have a closer look at the governance structure in the organization (see Graph 6.1).

The IMF Board of Governors is the highest decision-making body of the IMF. It consists of one governor and one alternate governor for each member country. The governor is appointed by the member country and is usually the minister of finance or the head of the central bank. The Board of Governors is responsible for personnel of the executive directors, and the membership in the organization. The Board of Governors retains the right to approve quota increases and SDRs allocations, in other words, to decide if and how much the total amount of SDRs is to be created.

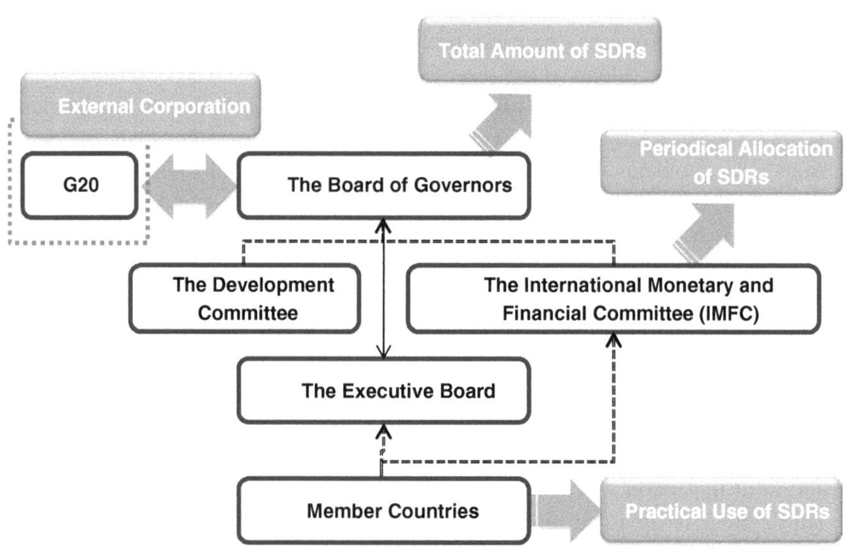

Graph 6.1 SDRs decision process

The Executive Board of the IMF is composed by 24-member which, together, represent all 187 countries. Large economies, such as the United States and China, have their own seat at the table while most other countries are grouped in constituencies. Each constituency represents from 4 to 24 countries. The Executive Board takes care of the daily business of the IMF.

The Board of Governors is advised by two committees, the International Monetary and Financial Committee (IMFC) and the Development Committee. The IMFC' structure mirrors that of the Executive Board and its 24 constituencies, thus representing all the member countries of the Fund. The IMFC meets twice a year and discusses matters of common concern affecting the global economy. Normally, the Committee issues a joint communiqué summarizing its views to the Board of Governors on when and how much SDRs should be supplemented to the system.

Another consultative committee, the Development Committee is a joint committee, representing the full membership of the IMF and the World Bank and mainly serves as a forum for building intergovernmental consensus on critical development issues.

There are still some inter-government institutions that give informal advices to IMF on SDRs or other monetary issues, such as G20 (G20 has substitutes G7/8 as a more inclusive and influential inter-government corporation platform on world economy).

According to the organizational structure and decision-making process in the IMF, it is the Board of Governors that decides the time and the amount of total SDRs to be created. More specifically, each constituency of the IMFC that represents certain number of countries discusses and proposes when and how the additional SDRs should be allocated. Their joint communiqué is reviewed and finally decided by the Board of Governors. Then, the Executive Board takes charge of implementation. However, each member owns the power to use the SDRs it receives, thus finally activating its system.

Allocations of the SDRs

Under its Articles of Agreement, the IMF may allocate SDRs to member countries in proportion to their IMF quotas. Such an allocation provides each member with a costless, unconditional international reserve asset. The SDRs mechanism is self-financing and levies charges on allocations which are then used to pay interest on SDRs holdings. If a member does not use any of its allocated SDRs holdings, the charges are equal to the interest received. However, if a member's SDRs holdings rise above its allocation, it effectively earns interest on the excess. Conversely, if it holds fewer SDRs than allocated, it pays interest on the shortfall. The Articles of Agreement also allow for cancellations of SDRs, but this provision has never been used. The IMF cannot allocate SDRs to itself or to other prescribed holders.

On January 1, 1970, a first 3 billion of SDRs were issued and allocated among members of the IMF. This particular amount was decided by such a prospect that a reserve shortage would be unavoidable as the US monetary policy tied down in 1969. Meanwhile, it also decided that another two additional allocations, each of the approximately amount as the first one, issued in the following two years: 2.9

billion in 1971 and 3.4 billion in 1972. Then in 1979–1981, 12.1 billion SDRs was allocated in yearly installment. By the end of August, 2009, to ensure sufficient liquidity and so to promote the world economy, SDRs allocation was historically up to 161.2 billion. Along with a special one-time allocation of SDRs 21.5 billion took effect in the same year, total cumulative allocations was brought to about SDRs 204 billion (equivalent to about $318 billion).

Every member of the IMF can receive a certain amount of the SDRs proportioned to its quota in the Fund. Moreover, the increased allocation of SDRs a country receives will be an asset that offsets the country's increased liability to its SDRs account. Since this decided allocation is independent of any considerations about the real external needs on liquidity of a country, member who suffers external imbalance could use its amount of SDRs as an instrument of adjustment.

Adjustment methods of the SDRs

After each member gets its initial amount of SDRs, it can choose to hold them as international reserves or to use them as a method of adjustment when the country runs an imbalance of its payments. For example, country A runs in a external deficit and it surely faces the risk of volatility in its foreign exchange market. By swapping its SDRs reserves into an equivalent amount of international money that it needs, country A gets the resource to intervene in its exchange market and keep its currency stable. On the other hand, there is a surplus country B willing to accept this amount of SDRs so as to make it possible to further diversify its intentional reserves portfolio, or simply gains the interests from the swap operation. In the case that there are not enough voluntary receptors of SDRs, the IMF can designate members with surplus position of their balance of payments to provide freely usable currency in exchange for SDRs. This so-called "designation mechanism" doubly ensures that a participant can use its SDRs to readily obtain an equivalent amount of currency if it has a need for such a currency. Therefore, the introduction of the SDRs was intended to establish a "giro system" aimed at stabilizing exchange rates (Machlup 1968).

Valuation of the SDRs

Although there is not any formal agreement, several principles are shared in common to be the guidance of valuating the SDRs since the 1970s for the proper of "enhancing the attractiveness of the SDRs as a reserve asset" (IMF 2010).

The current value of SDRs can be expressed as U.S. dollars per unit, and it is decided by the total value of a basket of certain international moneys that selected by the Board of Governors of the IMF. This standard basket method introduced in 1974, has been used as the method that "best ensures the stability of the SDRs in terms of the major currencies under floating exchange rates". Following the principles, the valuation of the SDRs should be "continuity in the method... such that revisions in the method of valuation occur only as a result of major changes in the roles of currencies in the world economy" (IMF 2010). So do the composition of the SDRs currency basket. According to the principles of stability and representativeness, the currencies included must be the major international moneys in the world and should be widely used in international transactions. In a word, "the relative weights of currencies included in the basket should reflect their relative importance in the world's trading and financial system" (IMF 2010).

So far, the SDRs valuation basket includes the US dollar, the euro, the Japanese yen and the British pound sterling. They were selected by the following criteria from the IMF: the SDRs basket comprises the four currencies that are issued by Fund members (or by monetary unions that include Fund members), whose exports of goods and services during the five-year period ending 12 months before the effective date of the revision had the largest value, and that have been determined by the Fund to be freely usable currencies in accordance with Article XXX (f), which reads:

A freely usable currency means a member's currency that the Fund determines (i) is, in fact, widely used to make payments for international transactions, and (ii) is widely traded in the principal exchange markets.

It is notable that the concept of a freely usable currency concerns the actual international use and trading of currencies, and is distinct from whether a currency is either freely floating or fully convertible (IMF 2010).

As for the currency weighting, the IMF also publishes the variables and the method:

The percentage weight of each currency selected shall reflect:

(a) Reserves; the value of the balances of that currency held by the monetary authorities of other members 10 at the end of each year of the relevant five-year period ending 12 months before the effective date of the revision; and
(b) Exports; the value of exports of goods and services of the members or monetary unions as defined in the method for currency selection.

The currencies and their weights in the valuation basket shall be reviewed every five years in order to keep the composition of the basket stable for at least that period of time, unless the Executive Board decides otherwise (IMF 2010).

Therefore, the method of valuating the SDRs is

1 SDRs = Σ (U.S. dollar equivalents of each Currency in the basket); and

*U.S. dollar equivalent of each Currency = Each Currency Amount * its Foreign Exchange Rate against dollar = Q*F*

If:
Q = Currency Amount, F = Foreign Exchange Rate against dollar;
U.S. dollar equivalent of Euro = QeFe;
U.S. dollar equivalent of Japanese yen = QjyFjy;
U.S. dollar equivalent of Pound sterling = QpFp;
U.S. dollar = Qd;
Then:
1 SDRs = QeFe + QjyFjy + QpFp + Qd

Of which, the Currency Amount is determined by the weight of each currency in the SDRs basket that reassessed every half a decade and based on average exchange rates for last three months. They adjust proportionally to ensure that the value of the

SDRs is the same before and after the revisions but remain unchangeable for the subsequent 5-year period. However, the actual value of the SDRs changes daily reflecting in time the changes in exchange rates.

Here, according to the latest review of the valuation method by the IMF, we get the example calculation of new weights of each currency average from 2005 to 2009 (see Sheet 6.1).

Then we can get their currency amount and the US dollar equivalent respectively (see Sheet 6.2).

Finally, we calculate a new valuation of SDRs in Jun 1st, 2011:

1 SDRs = 1.540034 USD

Price of the SDRs

The price of the SDRs, like any other international money, is expressed by its interest rate. The interest rate on the SDRs is based on the sum of the multiplicative products in SDRs terms of the currency amounts in the SDRs valuation basket, the level of the interest rate on the financial instrument of each component currency in the basket, and the exchange rate of each currency against the SDRs.

Sheet 6.1 New weights of each currency average from 2005 to 2009

	(1) Exports of goods and services	(2) Official holdings of currencies	(3) Total of Cols. (1) and (2)	(4) Weights in percentage of totals in Col. (3) (%)
	In billions of SDRs			
us	1473.60	1602.00	3075.60	41.95
Euro area	2092.04	647.00	2739.04	37.36
UK	720.90	105.00	825.90	11.26
Japan	614.86	77.00	691.86	9.44
Total	4901.40	2431.00	7332.40	100.00
Relative weight (%)	66.85	33.15	100.00	

Sheet 6.2 Calculation of currency amounts in the new SDRs basket (as of December 30, 2010)

Currency	Initial new weight (share)	Illustrative currency amount	Exchange rate on 12/30/10	U.S. dollar equivalent
Euro	37.4	0.4230	1.325000	0.560475
Japanese yen	9.4	12.1000	81.630000	0.148230
Pound sterling	11.3	0.1110	1.543500	0.171329
U.S. dollar	41.9	0.6600	1.000000	0.660000

It is crucial when international reserves swap or transactions happen. To make it more sensible and to avoid any arbitrage activities, the Executive Board has introduced some principles of selecting the benchmark: the financial instruments in the SDRs interest rate basket should be broadly representative of the range of financial instruments that are actually available to investors in a particular currency, and the interest rate on the instrument should be responsive to changes in underlying credit conditions in the corresponding money market; and have risk characteristics that are similar to the official standing of the SDRs itself, i.e., have a credit risk profile of the highest quality, fully comparable to that of government paper available in the market or, in the absence of appropriate official paper, comparable to the credit risk on prime financial instruments. Instruments should also reflect the actual reserve asset choice of reserve managers, for example, as regards the form of the financial instrument, its liquidity, and maturity (IMF 2010).

Certain benchmark rates has then been recognized and used as representative interest rates for the four currencies are as follows:

Three-month U.S. Treasury bills for the US dollar;
Three-month Eurepo for the euro;
Three-month Japanese Treasury Discount Bill for Japanese yen; and
Three-month U.K. Treasury bills for Pound sterling.
The yields on these instruments are used to calculate the SDRs interest rate for each week.

Interest Rate of SDRs = Σ (Equivalent Interest Rate of each Currency in the basket); and

*Equivalent Interest Rate of each Currency = Each Currency Amount * Each Benchmark of the Interest Rate * its Exchange Rate against the SDRs = Q*R*F*

If,
Q = Currency Amount, R = Benchmark of the Interest Rate, F = Foreign Exchange Rate against dollar;
Euro Equivalent Interest Rate = Qe Re Fe;
Japanese yen Equivalent Interest Rate = QjyRjyFjy;
Pound sterling Equivalent Interest Rate = QpRpFp;
U.S. dollar Equivalent Interest Rate = QdRd Fd;
Then,
Interest Rate of the SDRs = Qe Re Fe + QjyRjyFjy + Qd Rd Fd + Qd Rd Fd

Rule T-1 of the SDRs has been amended and specifies that the SDRs interest rate for each weekly period commencing each Monday shall be the higher of (i) the combined market interest rate or (ii) 0.050 %. The combined market interest rate is the sum, as of the Friday preceding each weekly period, rounded to three decimal places, of the products that result from multiplying each yield or rate listed above by the value in terms of SDRs of the amount of the corresponding currency specified in Rule O-1. If a yield or rate is not available for a particular Friday, the calculation shall be made on the basis of the latest available yield or rate.

Sheet 6.3 Calculation of SDRs interest rate (for the week of April 27, 2015 to May 03, 2015)

Currency	Currency amount (A)	Exchange rate against the SDRs (B)	Interest rate (C)	Product (A) × (B) × (C)
Euro	0.423	0.780681	−0.188384	−0.0622
Japanese yen	12.1	0.00603556	−0.02	−0.0015
U.K. pound sterling	0.111	1.09017	0.42	0.0508
U.S. dollar	0.66	0.72125	0.03	0.0143
Total				0.0014
Floor for SDRs interest Rate				0.05
SDRs interest rate				0.05

Previously, the SDRs interest rate was set equal to the combined market interest rate and rounded to two decimal places.

Again, we take SDRs Interest Rate Calculation using the data of the week of April 27 to May 03, 2015 as an example (see Sheet 6.3).

Here we get SDRs interest rate of that period is 0.05.

6.2 Another Way Worth Trying?

The SDRs was created by the IMF in 1969 to support the Bretton Woods fixed exchange rate system. A country participating in this system needed official reserves—government or central bank holdings of gold and widely accepted foreign currencies—that could be used to purchase the domestic currency in foreign exchange markets, as required to maintain its exchange rate. But the international supply of two key reserve assets—gold and the U.S. dollar—proved inadequate for supporting the expansion of world trade and financial development that was taking place. Therefore, the international community decided to create a new international reserve asset under the auspices of the IMF.

Only a few years after the creation of SDRs, the Bretton Woods system collapsed and the major currencies shifted to a floating exchange rate regime. In addition, the growth in international capital markets facilitated borrowing by creditworthy governments. Both of these developments lessened the need for SDRs. However, more recently, the 2009 SDRs allocations totaling SDRs 182.6 billion have played a critical role in providing liquidity to the global economic system and supplementing member countries' official reserves amid the global financial crisis.

6.2.1 *The Intrinsic Weakness of the SDRs*

No one can deny that the creation of the SDRs is a valuable trying which intended to solve the problem of the shortage and the volatility of the international reserves, especially after realizing the "Dilemma" caused by a national currency as an international standard in a fixed exchange rate regime. It is an unprecedented task for people to design and carry out such a high level of corporation on monetary affairs. So far, under the surveillance of the IMF, the SDRs have been placed great expectations for several times in history, as well as in the most recent crisis. However, "the historical record of SDRs as international reserves is altogether unimpressive" (Alessandrini and Fratianni 2009).

By the end of 1972, the SDRs constituted about 9.5 % of the world's stock of non-gold reserve assets. While before the latest general and special allocation, there were 21.4 billion SDRs in existence, accounting for less than 0.5 % of the total world (non-gold) reserves. These figures may show that the SDRs were not progressed as its planners expected. So we had better study closely and to find out its intrinsic weakness.

(1) *From quantitative aspect*

As we pointed above, a key difference between a dollar-centered system and a SDRs-centered system lies in the supply mechanism. Certain amount of SDRs is activated exogenously and independently by the IMF administration, beyond any specific consideration to countries' needs. Based on the classic economic theory, there is a view that the supply of money should respond to changes in demand so as to get the equilibrium point. In terms of an international reserve, this kind of automatically response helps countries to achieve their external adjustment. Alternatively, if the amount of SDRs supply is decided in certain period in addition with a fixed interest rate, it must be rigid for the countries to carry out their adjustment. Even though the IMF would make some necessary review and adjust the amount of quota, the lagging effects would make countries that are in need of the SDRs obtained the resource at a very high expense.

In fact, the arrangement of the SDRs supply reflected the economic philosophy behind it. The sharp division between monetarism versus Keynesianism lies in "whether the IMF should allocate SDRs so as to secure an equilibrium long-run monetary growth rate independent of short-run fluctuations in aggregate demand or whether it should try to engage in short-run countercyclical fine-tuning" (Williamson 2009). The monetarists won at that time, so the IMF went on determining the pace and the amount of SDRs allocations for "basic periods," on the basis of prospective shortages of reserves. However, as now when the world is in a serious recession, it appears that the authorities prefer to apply Keynesian "pump-priming" rather than following to the 1970s monetarist logic that SDRs should act strictly as a reserve supplement.

(2) *From qualitative aspect*

The credibility as an international reserve

It is argued that SDRs cannot be used to settle cross-border transactions or as a unit of value in which to denominate international bonds. This means that there are no private markets for SDRs. In all, SDRs are neither money nor a claim on any institution.

Secondly, this fact that the monetary authority would have to change them into some intervention currency before intervention would reduce its attractiveness as official holdings.

In other words, the SDRs are even not satisfied the criteria used for selecting the composited international moneys of its own: "A freely usable currency means a currency that is, in fact, widely used to make payments for international transactions, and is widely traded in the principal exchange markets."

The feasibility of adjustment

As we mentioned before, the SDRs system is created to help achieve some necessary adjustment when large imbalance occur. However, it proved from the history that the SDRs system did little to improve the situation between largest deficit member and its net debtor.

If the SDRs try to meet the needs for the US to do something to adjust, considering the huge size of its deficits, the additional allocation would be sole for the US. According to the planed working system of adjustment, the US swaps the huge allocation of SDRs for dollar assets in the net debtor countries like China. But as the US is and seems continue to be a provider of predominant international money, this kind of operation would have marginal effect on sterilization of the excessive supply of dollar. Actually, the US monetary base would be left unchanged.

Only to sell its T-bills that received from debtor in exchange of the SDRs could reduce the US monetary base. It is unclear that the Fed will voluntarily accept the SDRs instead of dollar-dominated assets.

6.2.2 A Bridge to Supranational Standard

The SDRs is neither a currency, nor a claim on the IMF. Rather, it is a potential claim on the freely usable currencies of IMF members. Holders of SDRs can obtain these currencies in exchange for their SDRs in two ways: first, through the arrangement of voluntary exchanges between members; and second, by the IMF designating members with strong external positions to purchase SDRs from members with weak external positions. In addition to its role as a supplementary reserve asset, the SDRs serves as the unit of account of the IMF and some other international organizations.

Although the nature of the SDRs might not be perfect, this vehicle currency is so far the most promising idea as well as experiment to solve the problem of "Triffin Dilemma" with the sovereign currency standard, and the trap with the regional single currency standard. But, to successfully performance as a bridge to a real and sound supranational standard, the SDRs should seriously consider at least two questions, each one should be the forthcoming goals for the reformation of the IMF.

The Transaction and the Usage

IMF members often need to buy SDRs to discharge obligations to the IMF, or they may wish to sell SDRs in order to adjust the composition of their reserves. The IMF may act as an intermediary between members and prescribed holders to ensure that SDRs can be exchanged for freely usable currencies. For more than two decades, the SDRs market has functioned through voluntary trading arrangements. Under these arrangements a number of members and one prescribed holder have volunteered to buy or sell SDRs within limits defined by their respective arrangements. Following the 2009 SDRs allocations, the number and size of the voluntary arrangements has been expanded to ensure continued liquidity of the voluntary SDRs market. The number of voluntary SDRs trading arrangements now stands at 32, including 19 new arrangements since the 2009 SDRs allocations.

In the event that there is insufficient capacity under the voluntary trading arrangements, the IMF can activate the designation mechanism. Under this mechanism, members with sufficiently strong external positions are designated by the IMF to buy SDRs with freely usable currencies up to certain amounts from members with weak external positions. This arrangement serves as a backstop to guarantee the liquidity and the reserve asset character of the SDRs.

The Allocation and the Valuation

General allocations of SDRs have to be based on a long-term global need to supplement existing reserve assets. Decisions on general allocations are made for successive basic periods of up to five years, although general SDRs allocations have been made only three times. The first allocation was for a total amount of SDRs 9.3 billion, distributed in 1970–72, the second—for SDRs 12.1 billion—distributed in 1979–81, and the third—for SDRs 161.2 billion—was made on August 28, 2009. Separately, the Fourth Amendment to the Articles of Agreement became effective August 10, 2009 and provided for a special one-time allocation of SDRs 21.5 billion. The purpose of the Fourth Amendment was to enable all members of the IMF to participate in the SDRs system on an equitable basis and rectify the fact that countries that joined the IMF after 1981—more than one fifth of the current IMF membership—never received an SDRs allocation until 2009.

The 2009 general and special SDRs allocations together raised total cumulative SDRs allocations to SDRs 204 billion. While in that year, GDP in China alone was up to 5000 billion U.S. dollar (which was more than SDRs 3000 billion). In fact, the current amount of SDRs allocation would surely far beyond the real needs of the world economy.

Secondly, as the book introduced above, the value of the SDRs was initially defined as equivalent to 0.888671 g of fine gold—which, at the time, was also equivalent to one U.S. dollar. After the collapse of the Bretton Woods system in 1973, the SDRs was redefined as a basket of currencies. Today the SDRs basket consists of the euro, Japanese yen, pound sterling, and U.S. dollar. The value of the SDRs in terms of the U.S. dollar is determined daily and posted on the IMF's website. It is calculated as the sum of specific amounts of the four basket currencies valued in U.S. dollars, on the basis of exchange rates quoted at noon each day in the London market.

The basket composition is reviewed every five years by the Executive Board, or earlier if the IMF finds changed circumstances warrant an earlier review, to ensure that it reflects the relative importance of currencies in the world's trading and financial systems. In the most recent review (in November 2010), the weights of the currencies in the SDRs basket were revised based on the value of the exports of goods and services, and the amount of reserves denominated in the respective currencies that were held by other members of the IMF. These changes became effective on January 1, 2011. In October 2011, the IMF Executive Board discussed possible options for broadening the SDRs currency basket. Most directors held the view that the current criteria for SDRs basket selection remained appropriate. The next review is currently scheduled to take place by the end of 2015.

Nowadays, more and more voice is calling for the inclusion of China to help reinforce the function of the SDRs as an international standard. China now is growing into another influential power in international monetary affairs. During the past five years, the process of CNY internationalization has been accelerating. Currently, CNY has ranked the world's second trade financing currency and the sixth transaction currency. It is recorded that a number of monetary authorities have applied CNY as their foreign reserve currency. Meanwhile, the development of CNY on-shore and off-shore markets, as well as the oversea deposits, debts and other financial derivatives together represent the CNY is going forward to a freely used international currency. Not to mention Its accumulatively huge amount of official reserves could play some decisive role in course to improve the world imbalance.

A case study: what would happen if including China with Current SDRs basket?

The first valuable trying is to find the results after inclusion of Chinese CNY with current system. In the term of "current system", it means two aspects of conditions are supposed to remain unchanged as the hypotheses:

One is the method of valuation of the SDRs is fixed, that is to say, the percentage weight of each currency reflect both the factor of the value of the balances of that currency held by the monetary authorities of other members ("Reserves") and of the value of exports of goods and services statue of the members or monetary unions ("Exports").

The other one is, Chinese yuan is at its current situation that far beyond a real international money with capital movement controls and pegged exchange rate against dollar.

On the basis of these hypotheses, we follow below steps to try to introduce Chinese yuan into SDRs basket. To be more comparable, we use the data of China in the currency weight calculation in the same period from 2005 to 2009 (see Sheet 6.4).

For the outstanding performance in international trade, especially in the field of exports, China counts for a large share of the "Exports" weight, surpassing the UK and Japan in the basket. On the other hand, however, almost zero of Chinese yuan is held by other members as an official reserve which proves so far that this currency is not "freely useable money" in the international monetary system. Anyway, according to the valuation method, we can get the new percentage of each currency in the basket, in which China accounts for 10.46 %, next to the U.S. and Euro area.

Secondly, each Currency Amount determined by the weight of each currency can be obtained, in which Chinese yuan shares 10.5, after the US dollar (37.6) and the Euro (33.4) (see Sheet 6.5).

Sheet 6.4 Inclusion of China with the current system (from 2005 to 2009)

	(1)	(2)	(3)	(4)
	Exports of goods and services	Official holdings of currencies	Total of Cols. (1) and (2)	Weights in percentage of totals in Col. (3) (%)
	In Billions of SDRs			
US	1473.50	1602.00	3075.60	37.56
Euro area	2092.04	647.00	2739.04	33.45
UK	720.90	105.00	825.90	10.09
Japan	614.86	77.00	691.86	8.45
China	**856.64**	**0.00**	**856.64**	10.46
Total	5758.04	2431.00	8189.04	100.00
Relative weight (%)	70.31	29.69	100.00	

Note China here is referred to China, P.R. (mainland China)
Source The World Bank

Sheet 6.5 Calculation of currency amounts in the new SDRs basket (as of December 30, 2010)

Currency	Initial new weight (share)	Illustrative currency amount	Exchange rate on 12/30/10	U.S. dollar equivalent
Euro	33.4	0.3783	1.325000	0.501184
Japanese yen	8.4	10.6793	81.630000	0.130826
Pound sterling	10.1	0.0983	1.543500	0.151674
U.S. dollar	37.5	0.5791	1.000000	0.579051
Chinese yuan	10.5	1.0769	6.622900	0.162600

Note The exchange rate for the Japanese yen and Chinese CNY are expressed in terms of currency units per U.S. dollar; other rates are expressed as U.S. dollars per currency unit

Finally, based on average exchange rates for last three months, we calculate a new valuation of SDRs included CNY in Jun 1st, 2011:

1 SDRs = 1.525336 USD

If, we modify a litter our hypotheses as follows,

Chinese yuan is still at its current situation that far beyond a real international money with capital movement controls and pegged exchange rate against dollar.

China enjoys a constantly high-speed of economic development which in turn proportionately increases its currency's global influence.

Other basket currencies experience synchronous development with each other so that the relative weight among them remains unchanged.

The method of weighting the basket money has changed some of its variables, as introducing GDP, stock market value and so on.

Sheet 6.6 Enlarge the weight of Chinese CNY

	Weights in percentage exclude RMB (%)	Weights in Percentage include RMB of 20 % (%)	Weights in Percentage include RMB of 30 % (%)
US	41.9	33.6	29.4
Euro area	37.4	29.9	26.1
JK	11.3	9.0	7.9
Japan	9.4	7.5	6.6
China	**N.A**	**20.0**	**30.0**
Total	100.0	100.0	100.0

Calculation of currency amounts in the new SDRs basket (as of December 30, 2010)

Currency	Initial new weight (share) (%)	Illustrative currency amount	Exchange rate on 12/30/10	U.S. dollar equivalent
If China accounts for 20 %				
Euro	29.9	0.3388	1.325000	0.448965
Japanese yen	7.5	9.5606	81.630000	0.117121
Pound sterling	9.0	0.0880	1.543500	0.135756
U.S. dollar	33.6	0.5162	1.000000	0.516218
Chinese yuan	20.0	2.0512	6.622900	0.309714
SDRs				1.527774
If China accounts for 30 %				
Euro	26.1	0.2965	1.325000	0.392844
Japanese yen	6.6	8.3655	81.630000	0.102481
Pound sterling	7.9	0.0770	1.543500	0.118787
U.S. dollar	29.4	0.4517	1.000000	0.451691
Chinese yuan	30.0	3.0768	6.622900	0.464571
SDRs				1.530373

(continued)

Sheet 6.6 (continued)

Currency	Initial new weight (share) (%)	Currency	Initial new weight (share) (%)	Currency	Initial new weight (share) (%)
Euro	33.4	Euro	29.9	Euro	26.1
Japanese yen	8.4	Japanese yen	7.5	Japanese yen	6.6
Pound sterling	10.1	Pound sterling	9.0	Pound sterling	7.9
U.S. dollar	37.6	U.S. dollar	33.6	U.S. dollar	29.4
Chinese yuan	**10.5**	**Chinese yuan**	**20.0**	**Chinese yuan**	**30.0**
SDRs	1.525336		1.527774	SDRs	1.530373

Now, suppose Chinese yuan is included in the basket and the currency amount is at the weight of 20 % or even 30 %, what would happen on the SDRs' new value? (see Sheet 6.6).

Firstly, there are some changes in the Currency Weights as shown in the sheet above. Then we can get new SDRs valuations respectively based on the changes of currency weights and the same average exchange rates.

It is surprised if we compare the three results of the SDRs' value: they are of highly similarity. It is obviously abnormal to general economic view because if one of the basket money enjoys a large share of increase which is based on its developed economic performance will lead to an appreciation of the SDRs whose value is determined by the basket of moneys, even if some introductions of new variables in the currency weighting.

Only one possibility to help answer this puzzle is: there is lack of a harmonious exchange rate regime among those basket moneys. If a currency (especially in the basket) is fixed at a certain level or pegged to particular currency (especially in the same basket), then it cannot reflect its real value in the international monetary system. Moreover, an international standard, such as SDRs, is agreed to be determined by a basket of international moneys because this sort of methodology is thought to help maximize the chance of stability of the value of the standard, in case of world imbalance occurs as we suffer today.

Therefore, it is time for the international community, especially for China, to consider a reestablishment of a stable international standard from the view of harmonizing the exchange rate regime.

Chapter 7
Conclusion

In 1944 at Bretton Woods, as a result of the collective conventional wisdom of the time, representatives from all the leading allied nations collectively favored a regulated system of fixed exchange rates, indirectly disciplined by a US dollar tied to gold–a system that relied on a regulated market economy with tight controls on the values of currencies.

Free trade relied on the free convertibility of currencies. Negotiators at the Bretton Woods conference, fresh from what they perceived as a disastrous experience with floating rates in the 1930s, concluded that major monetary fluctuations could stall the free flow of trade.

The new economic system required an accepted vehicle for investment, trade, and payments. Unlike national economies, however, the international economy lacks a central government that can issue currency and manage its use. In the past this problem had been solved through the gold standard, but the architects of Bretton Woods did not consider this option feasible for the postwar political economy. Instead, they set up a system of fixed exchange rates managed by a series of newly created international institutions using the U.S. dollar (which was a gold standard currency for central banks) as a reserve currency.

Flows of speculative international finance were curtailed by shunting them through and limiting them via central banks. This meant that international flows of investment went into foreign direct investment (FDI)–i.e., construction of factories overseas, rather than international currency manipulation or bond markets. Although the national experts disagreed to some degree on the specific implementation of this system, all agreed on the need for tight controls.

From 1947 until 1958, the U.S. deliberately encouraged an outflow of dollars, and, from 1950 on, it ran a balance of payments deficit with the intent of providing liquidity for the international economy. To encourage long-term adjustment, the U.S. promoted European and Japanese trade competitiveness. Gradually, Policies for economic controls on the defeated former Axis countries were scrapped. Aid to Europe and Japan was designed to rebuild productivity and export capacity. In the long run it was expected that such European and Japanese recovery would benefit the United States by widening markets for U.S. exports, and providing locations for U.S. capital expansion.

J. Wang, *The Past and Future of International Monetary System*,
SpringerBriefs in Economics, DOI 10.1007/978-981-10-0164-2_7

Bretton Woods, then, created a system of triangular trade: the United States would use the convertible financial system to trade at a tremendous profit with "developing" nations, expanding industry and acquiring raw materials. It would use this surplus to send dollars to Europe, which would then be used to rebuild their economies, and make the United States the market for their products. This would allow the other industrialized nations to purchase products from the Third World, which reinforced the American role as the guarantor of stability. When this triangle became destabilized, Bretton Woods entered a period of crisis that ultimately led to its collapse.

In 1960 Robert Triffin, Belgian American economist, noticed that holding dollars was more valuable than gold because constant U.S. balance of payments deficits helped to keep the system liquid and fuel economic growth. What would later come to be known as Triffin's Dilemma was predicted when Triffin noted that if the U.S. failed to keep running deficits the system would lose its liquidity, not be able to keep up with the world's economic growth, and, thus, bring the system to a halt. But incurring such payment deficits also meant that, over time, the deficits would erode confidence in the dollar as the reserve currency created instability.

Meanwhile, monetary interdependence made possible huge capital flows. As a result, official exchange rates often became unrealistic in market terms, providing a virtually risk-free temptation for speculators. They could move from a weak to a strong currency hoping to reap profits when a revaluation occurred. If, however, monetary authorities managed to avoid revaluation, they could return to other currencies with no loss. The combination of risk-free speculation with the availability of huge sums was highly destabilizing.

By 1968, the attempt to defend the dollar at a fixed peg of $35/ounce, had become increasingly untenable. Gold outflows from the U.S. accelerated. In 1967, the IMF agreed in Rio de Janeiro to replace the tranche division set up in 1946. Special drawing rights (SDRs) were set as equal to one U.S. dollar, but were not usable for transactions other than between banks and the IMF. Nations were required to accept holding SDRs equal to three times their allotment, and interest would be charged, or credited, to each nation based on their SDRs holding. The original interest rate was 1.5 %. The intent of the SDRs system was to prevent nations from buying pegged gold and selling it at the higher free market price, and give nations a reason to hold dollars by crediting interest, at the same time setting a clear limit to the amount of dollars that could be held. However, the Bretton Woods system was arguably doomed.

Some scholars argued that the demise of Bretton Woods System was driven by three key features of the macro backdrop:

- accelerating private capital flows,
- burgeoning imbalances,
- dramatically undervalued currencies, and three crucial catalysts: a sense of economic crisis, fears of a full-blown dollar collapse, and several bigger-than-life personalities.

It should be admitted that these features in place today are also prerequisites for the current international monetary system to collapse. And this is the background of the book.

7.1 Summary

In practice, the core components of an international monetary system should contain, among other things, the following three aspects: an international reserve standard played as an anchor in the system, some arrangements such as an agreed foreign exchange regime to help adjust each participant's international balance of payment, and accordingly global collaboration mechanism, like the practice from G7/8 to G20. All the three aspects are crucial for defining and evaluating an international monetary system. When it comes to understand the past and the current international monetary system so as to find out the right approach for the future one, it is quite sensible for this book to focus on those three components.

However, every crisis of International Monetary System is ultimately a crisis of the International Standards. From the Gold Standard, the Gold-exchange Standard, to the era of Paper Standard, it is acknowledged that the currency in the center of IMS represents the nature of the system. Similarly, the current international monetary system crisis reflects the result of some internal flaws of the current international standard. This book tries to explore the future of international monetary system through the basic logic: how do the intrinsic flaws of the current international standards constrain their functions on prompting the IMS in a more sustainable and balanced way?

As the Research Question, this paper is focused on different experiences of the current international standards, thus trying to understand what a sound international standard should be which is suitable for the future International Monetary System.

In Chaps. 3–5, the book focus on the current major moneys, the U.S. dollar, the euro and the CNY. As different experiences being a de facto international standard (or potentially), all the three could be grouped into:

- Sovereignty currency: equipped with "Triffin Dilemma" and "exorbitant privilege";
- Regional monetary integration: trapped by the contradictory development of economy and politics;
- Rising reserve currency: inexperienced with the pace of internationalization.

In the following Chapter of the book, the book puts forward the performance of the existent standard of international monetary system, the SDRs. Equally, the book first introduce the characteristics of its monetary system and its trial for acting as a supranational international standard. Moreover in this section, the book tries to experiment the inclusion of China CNY to the current SDRs system, to see the potential changes the system would have, thus proposing the SDRs' new reform.

The analytical research is mainly based on comparing the performance of major international standards in the current international monetary system. Their political/policy reactions and economic philosophies behind them are not only, to some extent, the reasonable response to the current international monetary system, but also fundamental factors for deciding the forth coming changes or reforms of a future international monetary system.

7.2 Added-Value of the Book

In the book, it is the first time to compare the different monetary system and their monetary performance of major currencies in the current international monetary system. Their political/policy reactions and economic philosophies behind them are not only, to some extent, the reasonable response to the current international monetary system, but also fundamental factors for deciding the forth coming changes or reforms of a future international monetary system.

The significance of my research, as presented in Chap. 2, is several-fold. Firstly, from a perspective of international monetary system to analyze the different monetary systems of major international standards. Secondly, by comparing the major international standards, the book tries to understand how the preference in the domestic monetary policy influence the performances of major currencies as intentional standard. Thirdly, it tries to emphasize the rise of CNY and its potential rising path. Ultimately, the purpose of studying on the book is to give rise to the question on how to put forward the feasible way to arrange a sound international monetary standard for the future international monetary system.

7.3 Limits of the Research Work and Future Research

There are several areas deserve to be worked on in future regarding to the International Monetary System, especially in the field of international standard.

Firstly, it is the role of the rising CNY. Through my research, it is provided that the monetary system and its characteristics of the currency and its backed economy. However, the more and more active domestic financial market as well as overseas, along with the needs to fulfill stable internationalization of its currency are all deserve to further study. For example, the CNY's enlarging off-shore market and its nearly geopolitical and economic proposes. To well prepare to accept a new "stake holder", going on researching about CNY and China will be necessary.

Secondly, as mentioned before, it is worth following up on the new round of reform in IMF, especially focusing on the SDRs' basket. Not only because this is the most suitable way for reestablishing a sound international standard and realizing accountable international coordination, but because this is so far the most promising experiment to realize the great conception by the architects of Bretton Woods system for a more stable international monetary system.

Bibliography

Beattie A (2011) Strength in reserve. Financial Times, 9 Feb 2011
Bénassy-Quéré A, Pisani-Ferry J (2011) What international monetary system for a fast-changing world economy. Bruegel working paper
Bergsten F (2009) Dollars and the deficit: how Washington can prevent the next crisis. Foreign Affair, November/December issue
Broz L (1997) The international origins of the federal reserve system. Cornell University Press, Ithaca
Calleo Y, Rowland BM (1973) American and world political economy. Indiana University Press, Bloomington
Chinese Capital Markets Development Report (2008) China Securities Regulatory Commission (ed)
Dadush U, Eidelman V (2010) How to avoid a currency war. Int Econ Bull (Carnegie Endowment for International Peace, 14 Oct)
Dooley M, Folkerts-Landau D, Garber P (2003) An Essay on the Revived Bretton Woods System. NBER Working Paper, No. 9971
Dooley M, Folkerts-Landau D, Garber P (2004) The revived Bretton woods system: the effects of periphery intervention and reserve management on interest rates & exchange rates in center countries. NBER Working Paper, No. 10332
Eichengreen B (1998) Exchange rate stability and financial stability. Open Econ Rev 9
Eichengreen B (2008) Globalizing capital: a history of international monetary system, 2nd edn. Princeton University Press, New Jersey
Eichengreen B (2009) Out of the box thoughts about the international financial architecture. IMF Working Paper WP/09/116
Eichengreen B (2010) Exorbitant privilege—the rise and fall of the dollar and the future of the international monetary system. Oxford University Press, Oxford
Eichengreen B, Frankel J (1996) The SDR, reserve currencies, and the future of the international monetary system. In: Michael M, James B, Peter I (eds) The future of the SDR in light of changes in the international financial system. International Monetary Fund
Farhi E, Gourinchas P-O, Rey H (2011) Reforming the international monetary system. Centre for Economic Policy Research
Fazio A (1998) The international monetary system. Open Econ Rev 9
Foundation B (2012) A study of China's national balance sheet. Social Sciences Academic Press (China), Beijing
Fratianni M et al (1998) Dominant currencies and the future of the euro. Open Econ Rev 9
Fratianni M, Salvatore D, Savona P (eds) (1999) Ideas for the future of the international monetary system. Kluwer Academic Publishers, Boston
Friedman M (1953) Essays in positive economics. University of Chicago Press, Chicago
Gochoco-Bautista MS (2010) To what extent should capital flows be regulated? The future global reserve system: an Asian perspective. Asian Development Bank

J. Wang, *The Past and Future of International Monetary System*,
SpringerBriefs in Economics, DOI 10.1007/978-981-10-0164-2

Hale D (1999) Will Europe's new currency threaten the US dollar and marginalize Japan's Yen? Zurich Group
IMF, World Economic Outlook
International Economics, Policy Brief, 09–20 Sept
Issing O et al (2010) Monetary policy in the euro area. China Financial Publishing House, Beijing
Jayakumar V, Weiss B (2011) Global reserve currency system: why will the dollar standard give way to a tripolar currency order? Front Econ China 6(1):92–130
Kenen P (2011) Beyond the dollar. J Policy Model 33(5):750–758
Krugman P (1984) The international role of the dollar: theory and prospect. In: Bilson J, Marston R (eds) Exchange rate theory and practice. University of Chicago Press, Chicago, pp 261–278
Lindert P (1969) Key currencies and gold: 1900–1913. Princeton Studies in International Finance, No. 24, Aug
McKinnon R (1979) Money in international exchange. Oxford University Press, New York
Meissner CM (2010) Systemic changes in the international monetary system and the need for coordination, cooperation and enforcement. In: Subacchi P, Driffill J (eds) Beyond, the dollar—rethinking the international monetary system. Chatham House, p. 57
Mishkin FS (2010) The economics of money, banking & financial market, 9th edn. China Renmin University Press, Beijing
Moghadam R (2011) Enhance international monetary stability—a role for the SDR? IMF working paper
Mundell RA (1995) The international monetary system: the missing factor. J Policy Modell 17 (5):479–492
Mundell RA (1961) A theory of optimum currency areas. Am Econ Rev 51(4):657–665
Mundell RA (1998) What the euro means for the dollar and the international monetary system. Atlantic Econ J 26(3):227–237
Mundell RA (2011) The case for restabilizing the international monetary systems. Lecture Delivered at Xiamen University, 5 Apr 2011
Nakao T (2010) Reforming the international monetary system: Japan's perspective. Symposium at the Institute for International Monetary Affairs, 18th March 2010. www.iima.or.jp/Docs/symposium/20100318/Mr_Nakao_Speech_text_e.pdf
Ocampo JA (2014) The provision of global liquidity: the global reserve system. World Institute for Development Economics Research. Working Paper 2014/141
Peng X (2010) The evolution of international monetary system and China's choice in the process of it's diversification, The Stanford Center for International Development. Working Paper 420
Pisani-Ferry J, Yu Y, Bénassy-Quéré A (2011) Reform of the international monetary system: some concrete steps. Bruegel Working Paper
Revived Bretton Woods System. NBER Working Paper No. 9971
Rosecrance R (1985) The rise of the trading state: commerce and conquest in the modern world. Basic Books Inc, New York
Saccomanni F (2000) Introduction: a new architecture or new system? A survey of international monetary reform in the 1990s. Open, Econ Rev 11
Salvatore D (2011) The future of tri-polar monetary system. J Policy Modell 33:776–785
Salvatore D (1998) International monetary and financial arrangements: present and future. Open, Econ Rev 9
Salvatore D (2000) The present international monetary system: problems, complications and reforms. Open Econ Rev
Savona P (2002) On some unresolved problems of monetary theory and policy. In: Michele F, Savona P, Kirton JJ (eds) Governing global finance—new challenges, G7 and IMF contributions. Ashgate Global Finance Series, Adelshot (Hampshire, UK), pp 177–183
Savona P (2007) Global development and the dollar: a conflict to be solved. In: Michele F, Savona P, Kirton JJ (eds) Financing development—the G8 and UN contribution. Ashgate Global Finance Series, Adelshot (Hampshire, UK), pp 241–251

Savona P (2010) On the macroeconomic effects of derivatives, English edn. Luiss University Press, Rome

Savona P (2011) The underlying money problem. Longitude, No 09

Savona P, Viviani C (2005) The impact on the U.S dollar of the conflict between the American Locomotive's model and the emerging economies' autopoietic growth. Presented at the third florence colloquium on the dollar and the quest for a new international monetary coordination. Organized by Associazione Guido Carli and Fondazione Cesifin in Florence on 23 Apr 2005

Savona P, Aurelio M (1998) On the relation between money and derivatives and its application to the international monetary market. Open, Econ Rev 9

Savona P (ed) (2000) The new architecture of the international monetary system. Kluwer Academic Publishers, Boston

Stiglitz J (2006) Making globalization work. W.W. Norton Press, New York

Stiglitz J, Member of a UN Commission Financial Expert (2010) Stiglitz report: reforming international monetary and financial system in the wake of global crisis. The New Press, New York

Subacchi P, Driffill J (2010) Introduction:no new Bretton woods,but a system in flux. In Subacchi P, Driffill J (eds) Beyond the dollar:rethinking the international monetary system, Chatham House, March 2010, p 1

Survey and Statistics, Statistics and Analysis Department of People's Bank of China. http://www.pbc.gov.cn/publish/diaochatongjisi/126/index.html

Swoboda AK (2000) Some challenges for reformers and architects. Open Econ Rev 11

Triffin R (1960) Gold and the dollar crisis. Yale University Press, New Haven

Truman EM (2009) The international monetary system and global imbalances. Present at a conference on the international monetary system: looking to the future and lessons from the past

Vines D (2010) European financial vulnerability and the need for a rules-based international monetary system. VoxEU.org, 4 June

Waltz K (1969) Man, the state and war. Columbia University Press, New York

Williamson J (2009) Why SDRs could rival the dollar. Peterson Institute for International Economics, 2009

Winkler A (2010) Exchange rate stabilization, network externalities and the discussion on a new key currency. In: Conference report linkages between international trade and financial markets, 17 and 18 June

Zhou X (2009) Reforming the international monetary system. BIS Rev 41

Zoellick R (2011) A monetary regime for a multipolar world. Financial Times, 17 Feb

陈建奇(Chen Jianqi) (2012) 破解'特里芬'难题——主权信用货币充当国际储备的稳定性 (Fight against 'triffin dilemma': the stability of the credit-based national currencies as international currencies). Econ Res J 10

黄薇 (Huang Wei) (2012) 全球经济治理之国际储备货币体系改革(Global economic governance: on the reform of international reserve currency). Stud Int Financ 12

李海英,石建勋 (Li Haiying, Shi Jianxun) (2012) 国外关于国际货币体系改革研究的最新动态 (Guowai Guanyu Guoji Huobi Tixi Gaige Yanjiu de Zuixin Dongtai). Soc Sc Abroad 2

罗伯特 蒙代尔 (Robert Mundell) (2012) 论国际货币体系的重建 (On the reconstruction of the international monetary system). J Xiamen Univ (Arts & Social Sciences) 1

盛斌,张一平 (Sheng Bin, Zhang Yiping) (2012) 全球治理中的国际货币体系改革:历史与现实 (The history and reality of the international monetary system reform in the global governance) Nan Kai J 1

田丰等(Tian Feng etc.) (2012) 全球失衡的内在根源 (A survey of global imbalances). J World Econ 10

王汉儒 (Wang Hanru) (2012) 后危机时代世界经济失衡根源与再平衡困局 (HouWeiji Shidai Shijie Jingji Shiheng Genyuan yu ZaiPingheng Kunju). Res Financ Econ Issues 5

徐梅(Xu Mei) (2012) 国际货币体系演变及我国应对政策选择 (On the evolution of international monetary system and China's counter). Pacific J 20(8)

MIX
Papier aus verantwortungsvollen Quellen
Paper from responsible sources
FSC® C105338

If you have any concerns about our products,
you can contact us on
ProductSafety@springernature.com

In case Publisher is established outside the EU,
the EU authorized representative is:
Springer Nature Customer Service Center GmbH
Europaplatz 3, 69115 Heidelberg, Germany

Printed by Libri Plureos GmbH
in Hamburg, Germany